hamlyn
QuickCook

hamlyn
QuickCook
Budget Meals

Recipes by Jo McAuley

Every dish, three ways—you choose!
30 minutes | 20 minutes | 10 minutes

An Hachette UK Company
www.hachette.co.uk

First published in Great Britain in 2012 by Hamlyn,
a division of Octopus Publishing Group Ltd,
Endeavour House, 189 Shaftesbury Avenue,
London, WC2H 8JY, UK
www.octopusbooks.co.uk

Distributed in the US by Hachette Book Group USA
237 Park Avenue, New York, NY 10017 USA
www.octopusbooksusa.com

Distributed in Canada by Canadian Manda Group
165 Dufferin Street, Toronto, Ontario, Canada M6K 3H6

ISBN 978-0-600-62405-9

Printed and bound in China.

10 9 8 7 6 5 4 3 2 1

Standard level spoon and cup measurements are used in all recipes unless
otherwise indicated.

Ovens should be preheated to the specified temperature. If using a convection oven,
follow the manufacturer's instructions for adjusting the time and temperature.
Broilers should also be preheated.

This book includes dishes made with nuts and nut derivatives. It is advisable for
those with known allergic reactions to nuts and nut derivatives and those who may
be potentially vulnerable to these allergies, such as pregnant and nursing mothers,
people with a chronic illness, the elderly, babies, and children, to avoid dishes made
with nuts and nut oils.

It is also prudent to check the labels of prepared ingredients for the possible inclusion
of nut derivatives.

The U.S. Department of Agriculture advises that eggs should not be consumed raw.
This book contains some dishes made with raw or lightly cooked eggs. It is prudent
for more vulnerable people, such as pregnant and nursing mothers, those with
weakened immune systems, the elderly, babies, and young children, to avoid dishes
made with raw or lightly cooked eggs.

Contents

Introduction

30 20 10—Quick, Quicker, Quickest

This book offers a new and flexible approach to planning meals for busy cooks, letting you choose the recipe option that best fits the time you have available. Inside you will find 360 dishes that will inspire and motivate you to get cooking every day of the year. All the recipes take a maximum of 30 minutes to cook. Some take as little as 20 minutes and, amazingly, many take only 10 minutes. With a little preparation, you can easily try out one new recipe from this book each night, and slowly you will build a wide and exciting portfolio of recipes to suit your needs.

How Does It Work?

Every recipe in the QuickCook series can be cooked one of three ways—a 30-minute version, a 20-minute version, or a superquick and easy, 10-minute version. At the beginning of each chapter, you'll find recipes listed by time. Choose a dish based on how much time you have and turn to that page.

You'll find the main recipe at the top of the page, accompanied by a beautiful photograph, as well as two time-variation recipes below.

If you enjoy the dish, you can go back and cook the other time options. If you liked the 20-minute Mixed Bean Pâté with Pine Nuts but only have 10 minutes to spare, then you'll find a way to cook it using speedy ingredients or clever shortcuts.

If you love the ingredients and flavors of the 10-minute Hot and Sour Chicken Salad, why not try something more substantial, such as the 20-minute Hot and Sour Chicken Soup, or be inspired to cook a more elaborate version, such as Hot and Sour Baked Chicken? Alternatively, browse through all of the 360 delicious recipes, find something that catches your eye—then cook the version that fits your time frame.

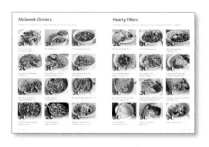

Or, for easy inspiration, turn to the gallery on pages 12–19 to get an instant overview by theme, such as Kids' Favorites or Cooking for a Crowd.

QuickCook Online

And to make life even easier, you can use the special code on each recipe page to e-mail yourself a recipe card for printing, or e-mail a text-only grocery list to your cell. Go to www.hamlynquickcook.com and enter the recipe code at the bottom of each page.

BUD-FISH-GES

QuickCook Budget Meals

This book is full of simple, appealing recipes that prove that you don't have to spend a fortune in order to eat delicious, nutritious home-cooked food. It is perfect for those of us who lead busy lives but still want to provide tasty meals for family and friends, without breaking the bank.

Cooking on a Budget

These simple hints and tips will help your money stretch farther at mealtime.

· **Pad it out** It's amazing how much farther you can make a meal go by throwing in some inexpensive carbohydrates or vegetables. For example, turning a lamb stew into a lamb and potato stew, or adding some small pasta shapes or lentils to a soup, can double the number of people it will feed. So pad a dish out, feed your family, and freeze the leftovers for another meal.

· **Cook in bulk** Not only is it cheaper to buy and cook in quantity, but it's easier, too. Try making up big batches of bolognese, chili, casseroles, and soups, and then freeze in portions. As well as cutting down on the time spent in the kitchen and the running costs of turning on the oven every night, this also means that you always have a quick, easy meal on hand. By the time you have ordered your takeout, you could already be serving a delicious, cheap homemade dinner ... the ultimate fast food!

· **Don't waste it!** Before you throw things away, try to think if there are other ways you could use them. For example, save bones or vegetable peels to make stocks, or put an empty vanilla bean in a jar of sugar to make vanilla sugar.

· **Make your own** So much of what we pay for is preparation and packaging. Buy loose vegetables that haven't been prewashed and trimmed, and meat that hasn't been cubed or cut into strips. Buy big bags of spices and herbs from health-food stores and ethnic food stores. They work out much cheaper and allow for you to make your own spice mixes, such as Mexican or Indian, much more cost effectively than buying them already prepared.

· **Experiment!** If you don't have exactly the same ingredients that the recipe calls for, then modify and tailor it to what you do have. Don't rush out to buy one type of pasta shape if you

have another in the pantry. Being on a budget doesn't
mean you can't be as creative and inventive as you desire!

Think Creatively

There is no denying that supermarkets are convenient, but
there are other places to acquire food if you think creatively.

· **Grow your own** Whether you are lucky enough to have
the space for a full-size vegetable patch, a small balcony for
growing in containers, or just a small windowsill for herbs,
by growing your own produce you will be doing much more
than saving money. You will know where your food has come
from; be helping the environment by reducing food miles; feel
enormous satisfaction as soon as those first shoots appear;
and eating tastier, more nutrient-packed vegetables. Picking
your vegetables and herbs just before eating them ensures
that they retain as many nutrients and vitamins as possible.
Try to form a gardening club with friends, so that everyone
can grow as much as possible and share their bumper crops
of tomatoes, zucchini, or beans, saving money for everyone.
If you don't have much space but want to grow more than
just a pot of herbs, look into a community gardening project.

· **Take a trip to the farmers' market** Many cities and large
towns have a weekly farmers' market. Try to time your trip
as the dealers are starting to pack up. Whether it's the
butcher, cheese merchant, or a fruit and vegetable farmer,
there will be items that they will want to get rid of, and there
are often great bargains on locally grown, seasonal produce.
You will usually need to cook them on the day, but with proper
planning that should not be a problem.

· **Be adventurous** Cooking and eating on a budget doesn't
mean having to stick to the same old boring meals day in and
day out, or buying from the same discount stores. Look at
other places where you might be able to buy cheaply. Buying
directly from the farm, for example, can work out cheaper
because there are no overheads involved in the transport and
selling of the goods. Cutting out the middleman in this way
means that the farms will often be able to sell at a more
advantageous price to you. This applies not just to fruit and
vegetables, but also to eggs and meat. If it means having to
buy large quantities, then get together with friends or family
and split the purchase between you, saving money for everyone.

- **Don't go shopping!** Well, obviously, you'll still have to go shopping some of the time, but why not try a bit of foraging? A nice long walk in the countryside doesn't just clear the head—it can also fill your basket. Blueberries, mushrooms (only if you are an expert in identifying mushrooms), and nuts are just a few of the things that can be found growing in our wildnerness … and all are free. Those blueberry muffins will never have tasted so good!

Hints and Tips for Smart Shopping

With a few tricks up your sleeve, a trip to the stores will result in bags full of the most useful and best-value produce available, and no unnecessary impulse buys to break the budget.

- **Make a list** Meal planning might sound a bit boring, but writing a list and sticking to it really does save money. Check out any promotional offers beforehand and incorporate them into your weekly planning so that you can use as many reduced-price ingredients as possible. When deciding what you will cook for the week, try to work out what ingredients you will have left over from one meal so that you can use it for the next. This will save money and avoid waste.

- **Never go shopping on an empty stomach** Unless you have willpower of steel, going food shopping with a grumbling belly is a recipe for disaster! There are just too many easy, tempting, and usually expensive items offered that could quickly blow your budget. Eat before you shop so that you won't be persuaded to purchase unnecessary items for snacking; if you are still tempted, then choose healthier snacks, which will keep you fuller for longer.

- **Beware of cheap meat** Cutting down on the quantity of meat in your diet is a quick way of saving money, but don't cut down on quality. If it's cheap, then it is probably at the expense of the animals' welfare, or because it has been pumped with water prior to being packaged. Try eating meat less often and having meat-free days, or opt for the cheaper, lesser-known cuts so that you can still enjoy meat without breaking the bank. For guidance, talk to your butcher, who will be happy to give advice.

- **Buy meat that has had as little preparation done to it as possible** Buying a whole chicken, for example, works out much less expensive than buying two legs, breasts, and wings. Not only is it cheaper, but once you have learned how to cut up a chicken yourself, you will be left with the carcass for making a great soup or stock.

· **Check the "reduced" section of the meat aisle** You may find organic, free-range meat at a fraction of the price because it is approaching its expiration date. Cook it that night, or freeze it on the day of purchase for another occasion.

· **Buy in bulk, cook in bulk** Buying ingredients in bulk may feel more expensive at the time, but you are actually saving money in the long run, because the price per pound works out lower. If you combine that with buying while products are on sale, you can make a real difference financially. If you buy fresh produce in bulk, then make sure it can be frozen to avoid waste.

· **Buy on sale** All supermarkets these days have good money-saving offers, such as "buy one, get one free," or products at half price. If the sales are on things that will actually provide a meal that you can enjoy, make the most of them by purchasing the items while they're being promoted, but be careful that you don't end up buying luxury items that you don't need.

· **Substitute** Replace prosciutto with another European-style cured ham, and Parmesan cheese with another hard Italian cheese; a lot of items have cheaper substitutes that are actually perfectly acceptable. Many European products are restricted by labeling laws but there are often others produced in a similar way to their more expensive counterparts.

Try seeking out cheaper alternatives, such as buying knobbly fruit and vegetables instead of perfect-looking ones—they will still taste the same and when cooked will look the same. Luxury items, such as smoked salmon, can be bought for a fraction of the price in the form of smoked-salmon trimmings. The same can be said for meat—ask your butcher if he has any odds and ends that he is willing to part with cheaply.

Substitute supermarket own-brand produce for the better-known, more expensive brands. It works out less expensive, and the quality is often the same.

· **Go abroad** If you live in or near a large town or city, take a "trip overseas" by shopping in ethnic stores. Chinese, Italian, Indian, Polish, Thai, Turkish ... the list is endless, and the produce is often much cheaper and fresher. It's possible to buy huge bunches of fresh herbs for very little, so bag a bargain and inspiration by varying where you shop.

Kids' Favorites

Kids can be hard to please, but these new favorites will be winners with all the family.

**Tandoori Chicken Wings
with Raita** 56

**Aloo Tikki with Cilantro
and Mint Chutney** 94

**Tomato and Mascarpone
Penne Pasta** 98

Homemade Baked Beans 116

**Macaroni and Cheese
with Bacon** 140

**Lamb Stew with
Mashed Potatoes** 154

**Pork Balls with
Sweet-and-Sour Sauce** 164

**Tuna Rissoles with
Coriander Mayonnaise** 184

**Lemon Grilled Fish with
Cheesy Mashed Potato** 212

**Crunchy Baked Apples
and Pears** 238

Old-Fashioned Rock Cakes 252

Almost Instant Peach Trifle 276

Cooking for a Crowd

When there are plenty of mouths to feed, practicality and value for money are the keys to success.

Mixed Bean Pâté with Pine Nuts 30

Meze Plate 42

Lemon and Spinach Soup with White Rice 60

Creamy Mushroom and Tarragon Rigatoni 76

Sweet Potato and Coconut Rice 82

Bulgur Wheat with Goat Cheese and Red Onion 84

Lentil Bolognese 114

Chunky Vegetable and Cheese Gratin 118

Chorizo and Lima Bean Salad 134

Creamy Cider Chicken with Rice 152

Spiced Shortbread Squares with Caramel Ice Cream 254

Ginger and Lemon Cupcakes 266

Winter Warmers

These comforting dishes are designed to warm heart, soul, and body.

Tomato and Chickpea Stew 26

Creamy Wild Mushroom Soup 36

Ham and Pea Soup with Crispy Bacon 48

Giant Tomato and Rosemary Muffins 52

Tomato, Bean, and New Potato Gratin 80

Mustardy Squash, Carrot, and Sweet Potato Casserole 92

Beef Pies with Crunchy Topping 148

Sausages with Mashed Potatoes and Celeriac 150

Baked Eggplant with Lamb and Pine Nuts 178

Melting Chocolate Desserts 248

Caramel Apples 250

Pear and Walnut Muffins 264

Summer Specials

Welcome the summer with some hot flavors and sizzling salads, perfect for lazy meals al fresco.

**Roasted Chickpeas
with Spinach** 68

**Ginger and Cilantro
Turkey Burgers** 128

Cajun-Spiced Hot Dogs 156

**Double Whammy Hamburgers
with Pickles** 158

**Turkey Milanese with Garlic
Mayonnaise and Garlic Bread** 162

**Shrimp and Avocado
Tostada** 186

**Teriyaki Salmon Sticks
with Bean Sprout Salad** 196

**Blackened Sardines
with Yogurt Dressing** 206

**Creamy Mustard and Trout
Pasta Salad** 208

**Spiced Mackerel and
Couscous Salad** 220

**Lemon Tart with
Vanilla Cream** 262

**Raspberry Ripple
Pain Perdu** 274

Impress Your Guests

Elegant meals don't have to break the bank, nor do they have to take hours to prepare.

**Hot-and-Sour
Chicken Salad** 38

**Creamy Baked Eggs
with Blue Cheese** 58

**Pork Schnitzel with Feta and
Lima Bean Salad** 130

**Fried Steak with Green
Peppercorn Sauce** 142

Baked Chicken with Lime 144

**Pan-Fried Gnocchi and
Chorizo Salad** 170

**Thai-Flavored Mussels
with Coconut Milk** 198

**Chile Crab and Rice Cakes
with Lime Dipping Sauce** 210

**Garlic Breaded Salmon with
Scallion Mashed Potatoes** 228

Chocolate and Nut Fondue 234

Sweet Almond Frittata 240

Quick Cherry Tiramisu 258

Ten-Minute Wonders

When you're running out of time or energy, these easy options will feed the family with minimal fuss.

Quick Quesadillas 24

Cauliflower Coleslaw
Pockets 62

Zucchini, Garlic, and
Chile Fusilli 78

Feta, Scallion, and
Walnut Mini Tarts 96

Brie and Thyme Melts 100

Warm Tomato, Liver,
and Bacon Salad 146

Chile and Anchovy
Dressed Pasta 200

Smoked Trout and
Rice Noodle Salad 214

Lemony Tuna and
Cranberry Bean Salad 222

Strawberry Yogurt Crunch 242

Banana and Caramel
Pancakes 246

Almond Affogato 272

Midweek Dinners

These comforting dishes are a pleasure to cook and eat after a busy day.

**Warm Mushrooms
with Potato Pancake** 28

Patatas Bravas 40

Chicken Noodle Broth 50

**Chorizo and Roasted
Red Pepper Tortilla** 54

**Baked Bell Peppers with
Feta and Scallions** 104

**Vegetable Noodles with
Stir-Fry Sauce** 120

**Pork, Mushroom, and
Lemon Tagliatelle** 136

**Sesame Chicken
and Noodles** 172

Ham and Mushroom Risotto 174

**Simple Sausage, Bean, and
Vegetable Stew** 176

**Skillet Pizza with
Anchovies** 194

**Spaghetti with Broccoli,
Lemon, and Shrimp** 216

Hearty Fillers

These hearty dishes are filling and satisfying and won't disappoint a healthy appetite.

All Day Breakfast Wrap 34

Chili con Verduda 88

Spicy Kidney Beans
with Rice 110

Farmhouse Meatballs
with Couscous 126

Keema Matar with
Mango Chutney 132

Pork Chops with Mashed
Parsnips and Apples 160

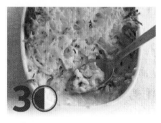

Easy Fish Casserole with
Crunchy Potato Topping 190

Fried Fish with Homemade
French Fries and Peas 204

Crunchy-Topped Cod and Leek
Pasta Casserole 226

Creamy Vanilla
Rice Pudding 244

Ginger and Syrup
Sponge Cake 256

Fallen Fruit Crisp 270

QuickCook

Soups and Snacks

Recipes listed by cooking time

10

Quick Quesadillas

Serves 4

1 cup refried beans
8 soft flour tortillas
¼ cup drained and chopped
  jalapeño pepper slices
1 large tomato, seeded
  and diced
1¼ cups shredded cheddar cheese
2 scallions, sliced
1 tablespoon finely chopped fresh
  cilantro (optional)
½ cup sour cream, to serve
  (optional)

- Spread the refried beans over 4 of the tortillas. Top with the jalapeño slices, diced tomato, cheddar, scallions, and chopped cilantro, if using. Cover each one with another tortilla to make 4 quesadillas.

- Toast the quesadillas, one at a time, in a large, ridged griddle pan over medium-high heat for 30–60 seconds on each side, until lightly browned and the cheese inside has melted.

- Cut the quesadillas into quarters and serve immediately with sour cream, if using.

Quesadilla-Style Pizzas Warm the refried beans and spread half over 4 large tortillas. Top each with a second tortilla, then spread the remaining beans on top. Place on 2 large baking sheets, and top with the jalapeño slices, diced tomato, sliced scallions, and 1 (15 oz) can kidney beans that have been drained, rinsed, and warm through. Sprinkle with the cheese and cook in a preheated oven, at 400°F, for 10–12 minutes, until the cheese is melted and bubbling. Cut into slices and serve hot with sour cream, chopped cilantro (if using), and shredded iceberg lettuce.

Spicy Bean Burritos Spread the refried beans over all 8 tortillas, then top with the jalapeño slices, 2 large, diced tomatoes, 1 chopped red bell pepper, and the sliced scallions. Tuck in the ends and roll each tortilla tightly, then place in a snug-fitting ovenproof dish. Pour 1 cup of store-bought hot Mexican salsa over the tortillas, then dot with small spoonfuls of sour cream and sprinkle with the cheese. Cook in a preheated oven, at 425°F, for 20–25 minutes, until hot and bubbling. Serve hot with shredded iceberg lettuce and chopped cilantro, if using.

 Tomato and Chickpea Stew

Serves 4

2½ tablespoons olive oil
1 large onion, chopped
1 green bell pepper, chopped
1 garlic clove, chopped
1-inch piece of fresh ginger root,
    peeled and chopped
1 teaspoon ground cumin
1 teaspoon ground coriander
2 tablespoons tomato paste
1 cups hot vegetable stock
4 large tomatoes, each cut into
    8 wedges
2 (15 oz) cans chickpeas, drained
    and rinsed
salt and pepper
2 tablespoons chopped flat leaf
    parsley, to garnish

- Heat the oil in a large, heavy saucepan or casserole. Add the onion, pepper, garlic, and ginger, and cook for 6–7 minutes, until softened.

- Stir in the ground spices and cook for an additional minute. Add the tomato paste, vegetable stock, tomato wedges, and chickpeas, then cover and bring to a boil. Season generously, reduce the heat, and simmer for about 8 minutes, until thickened slightly and the tomatoes have softened.

- Ladle into 4 warm bowls and serve garnished with the chopped parsley.

 Tomato, Chickpea, and Spinach Salad

Cook 3 thinly sliced scallions, 1 chopped red bell pepper, and the garlic and ginger, following the main recipe, adding the ground spices for the final minute. Dice the tomatoes and place in a large bowl with the chickpeas, 4 handfuls of baby spinach leaves, and the parsley. Season and add the cooked vegetables. Toss well together, divide among 4 shallow bowls, and serve immediately.

 Tomato and Chickpea Soup

Cook the onion, bell pepper, garlic, and ginger as above. Add the vegetable stock, tomato wedges, 1 (15 oz) can chickpeas, drained, and 2 cups tomato puree. Season generously and simmer gently for 15 minutes. Use a handheld immersion blender to blend the mixture until smooth. Ladle into 4 warm bowls and serve with a spoonful of plain yogurt and the chopped parsley to garnish.

30 Warm Mushrooms with Potato Pancake

Serves 4

3 potatoes (about 1¼ lb),
   scrubbed but unpeeled
½ onion, very thinly sliced
¼ cup vegetable oil
4 tablespoons butter
1 garlic clove, chopped
3½ cups thinly sliced
 button mushrooms
2 tablespoons finely chopped
   parsley (optional)
salt and pepper
1 large bunch of watercress,
   to serve

- Cook the potatoes whole in a large saucepan of lightly salted boiling water for 8–10 minutes. Drain and set aside to cool slightly. Wearing rubber gloves to protect your hands from the heat, coarsely shred the potatoes and mix in a bowl with the sliced onion, 2 tablespoons of the oil, and plenty of salt and pepper.

- Heat the remaining oil in a large nonstick skillet and add the potato mixture, pushing down to flatten it so that it covers the bottom of the skillet. Cook for 7–8 minutes, then slide onto an oiled plate or board. Flip the pancake back into the skillet to cook the other side for 7–8 minutes, until crisp and golden.

- Meanwhile, melt the butter in a skillet and cook the garlic and mushrooms gently for 6–7 minutes, until softened and golden. Season with salt and pepper, then stir in the chopped parsley, if using.

- Cut the potato pancake into wedges, then arrange on serving plates, sprinkle with the watercress, and spoon over the warm mushrooms with their juices. Serve immediately.

---

1 Garlic Mushrooms on Toast Melt the butter and sauté the garlic and mushrooms, following the main recipe. Heat a ridged grill pan and toast 4 large slices of sourdough or rustic-style bread until crisp and charred. Top with the watercress and spoon the hot garlic mushrooms over the toast. Serve immediately.

2 Warm Mushroom, Potato, and Watercress Salad Cook 1½ lb new potatoes in a large saucepan of lightly salted boiling water for 12–15 minutes, until tender. Meanwhile, heat 2 tablespoons oil in a large skillet and cook the sliced onion gently with the garlic for 7–8 minutes, until softened and golden. Stir in the mushrooms and cook for an additional 3–4 minutes, until tender. Drain the potatoes well, then add to the skillet with the chopped parsley and toss in the buttery juices for 1–2 minutes to coat. Toss with the watercress and serve immediately.

# Mixed Bean Pâté with Pine Nuts

Serves 4

2 tablespoons olive oil

1 large red onion, chopped

1 garlic clove, chopped

½ teaspoon hot smoked paprika

2 tablespoons pine nuts

2 cups drained and rinsed canned mixed beans, such as kidney beans, cranberry beans, pinto beans, and/or chickpeas

1 teaspoon lemon juice

2 tablespoons chopped chives

3–4 tablespoons plain yogurt

salt and pepper

- Heat the oil in a nonstick skillet and cook the onions for 5 minutes, then add the garlic and cook for an additional 3 minutes, until soft and golden. Add the smoked paprika for the final 30 seconds, then remove from the heat.

- Meanwhile, toast the pine nuts in a small, dry skillet for 2–3 minutes, until lightly golden, shaking the skillet frequently to prevent them from burning.

- Transfer the beans to a food processor with the lemon juice, half the chives, and the onion mixture. Season well, then blend briefly, adding enough yogurt to make a coarse-textured pâté.

- Spread the pâté onto hot toast and sprinkle with the toasted pine nuts and remaining chives. Serve immediately with celery sticks.

Quick Bean Pâté Place the beans in the food processor with ¼ cup cream cheese with chives, ½ teaspoon dried onion powder, and a pinch of dried garlic powder. Blend briefly to create a coarse-textured pâté, then season and spread on hot toast. Sprinkle with the smoked paprika, toasted pine nuts, and 1 tablespoon fresh chives, if desired.

Roasted Mixed Bean Salad Cut the red onion in half and slice into thin wedges. Toss with the beans, garlic, paprika, 3 tablespoons olive oil, and seasoning. Transfer to a roasting pan and cook in a preheated oven, at 400°F, for 20–25 minutes, until golden. Meanwhile, toast the pine nuts following the main recipe. Mix ⅔ cup plain yogurt with the chives and lemon juice, and season well. Remove the beans from the oven, let cool for 5 minutes, then toss with 1 (5 oz) package arugula leaves. Divide among 4 shallow dishes, sprinkle with the pine nuts, and serve immediately with the yogurt dressing.

Swiss Cheese Melts

Serves 4

1 large French baguette
2 cups shredded Swiss cheese
1 tablespoon whole-grain
  mustard
2 tablespoons mayonnaise
2 tomatoes, seeded and chopped
pinch of black pepper
1 small lettuce, leaves separated,
  to serve (optional)

- Cut the French baguette in half, then slice each half horizontally to form 4 long pieces.

- Place the shredded cheese in a bowl with the remaining ingredients and mix well to combine.

- Spoon the topping over the cut side of each piece of bread and place on a baking sheet. Cook under a preheated hot broiler for 3–4 minutes, until golden and bubbling. Serve hot with lettuce, if desired.

 ### Swiss Cheese Pasta Sauce

Slice 1 large onion and cook gently in 2 tablespoons vegetable oil for 6–7 minutes, until soft and golden. Stir in 1 tablespoon whole-grain mustard, 2 seeded and chopped tomatoes, 1¼ cups heavy cream, and 2 cups shredded Swiss cheese. Season well with salt and pepper, then stir over gentle heat until the cheese has melted. Serve over cooked pasta, accompanied by a crusty French baguette.

Swiss Cheese and Tomato Tart

Roll out 1 rectangular sheet of store-bought puff pastry. Mix together 1 tablespoon whole-grain mustard and 2 tablespoons mayonnaise, then spread thinly over the pastry, leaving a ¾-inch border. Slice 3 tomatoes thinly and arrange over the mustard mixture. Sprinkle with 2 cups shredd Swiss cheese, then sprinkle with 1 teaspoon dried mixed herbs. Bake in a preheated oven, at 400°C, for about 20 minutes, until the pastry is crisp and golden. Serve in slices with the lettuce.

 # All Day Breakfast Wrap

Serves 4

1 tablespoon vegetable oil,
plus extra for greasing
12 oz bulk sausage (or sausage
meat removed from the
casings)
3½ cups sliced button mushrooms
2 extra-large eggs
2 tomatoes, seeded and diced
4 large soft flour tortillas
salt and pepper
barbecue sauce or ketchup,
to serve (optional)

- Preheat the oven to 400°F and lightly grease a baking sheet. Divide and shape the bulk sausage into 4 long, flat sausages. Place on the baking sheet and cook in the preheated oven for 15–18 minutes, turning once, until cooked through.

- Meanwhile, heat the oil in a skillet and cook the mushrooms for 4–5 minutes, until softened and golden. Transfer to a bowl and keep warm. Place the skillet back over medium heat.

- Crack the eggs into a bowl and beat lightly. Stir in the chopped tomato, season with salt and pepper, and pour into the hot skillet. Stir gently until it starts to set, then cook for 1–2 minutes, until the bottom is golden and the omelet is just set. Slide onto a cutting board and slice thickly.

- Place 1 baked sausage in the center of each tortilla, then top with some mushrooms and strips of omelet. Roll tightly and cut in half diagonally. Serve hot with barbecue sauce or ketchup, if desired.

 All Day Breakfast French Toast Halve 2 tomatoes, drizzle with oil, and place cut side up on a foil-lined broiler rack with 8 bacon slices. Cook under a preheated broiler for 8–10 minutes, turning the bacon once, until the bacon is crisp and the tomatoes are slightly softened. Meanwhile, beat 4 eggs with 3 tablespoons milk and season. Dip 4 slices of bread in the egg mixture. Heat 2 tablespoons oil in a skillet and add the bread. Cook for 7–8 minutes, turning once, until golden. Serve immediately with the broiled bacon and tomatoes.

 All Day Breakfast Tortilla Place 8 sausage patties on a foil-lined broiler rack and cook under a preheated broiler for 10–12 minutes, turning occasionally, until cooked through. Meanwhile, heat the oil in a large skillet and cook 5 oz chopped bacon for 5–6 minutes, until golden. Add the sliced mushrooms and cook for an additional 4–5 minutes. Beat 5 eggs lightly and season with black pepper. Add to the skillet and stir occasionally until it begins to set. Slice the tomatoes thickly, then remove the sausages from the broiler. Arrange the sausages and tomatoes over the tortilla, and cook under a moderate broiler for an additional 3–4 minutes, until set and golden. Serve cut in wedges with hot, buttered toast.

3️⃣ Creamy Wild Mushroom Soup

Serves 4

½ oz dried wild mushrooms
½ cup boiling water
2 tablespoons butter
2 tablespoons olive oil
4 shallots or 1 onion, chopped
1 trimmed celery stalk, sliced
1 large potato (about 8 oz),
  peeled and diced
1 large garlic clove, finely chopped
1 lb mushrooms, coarsely
  chopped
3 cups hot vegetable stock
2–3 tablespoons light cream
salt and pepper
1 tablespoon chopped chives,
  to garnish
crusty bread, to serve (optional)

- Place the dried mushrooms in a bowl with the measured boiling water, then cover and set aside to soak.

- Heat the butter and olive oil in a large saucepan or casserole. Add the shallots, celery, potato, and garlic, and cook gently for about 10 minutes, until softened.

- Squeeze the excess moisture from the soaked mushrooms and chop finely, reserving the soaking liquid. Add both soaked and fresh mushrooms to the pan and cook for an additional 4–5 minutes, until softened.

- Strain the reserved soaking liquid into the pan along with the vegetable stock, and simmer gently for 8–10 minutes. Remove the pan from the heat and use a handheld immersion blender to blend until smooth. Season to taste with salt and pepper, then stir in the cream. Ladle into 4 deep bowls. Garnish with chopped chives, sprinkle with extra black pepper, and serve with crusty bread, if desired.

1️⃣ Creamy Mushroom Ciabatta Melt 2 tablespoons butter in a skillet. Cut 1 lb mushrooms in half, add to the skillet, and cook for 5–6 minutes, until soft and golden. Stir in ⅔ cup light cream, plenty of salt and pepper, and 1 tablespoon chopped parsley or chives, and cook for an additional minute. Toast 4 chunky slices of ciabatta or rustic-style bread on a grill pan and top with the mushroom mixture. Serve immediately.

2️⃣ Creamy Wild Mushroom Stroganoff Place ½ oz dried wild mushrooms, 4 shallots, and 1 large garlic clove in a mini chopper and process until minced. Cook in a skillet with 2 tablespoons each of butter and olive oil for 4–5 minutes, until softened. Add 4 cups thickly sliced mushrooms and cook for an additional 2–3 minutes. Then add ½ cup dry white wine and 1 cup heavy cream, and simmer gently for 6–7 minutes. Stir in 2 tablespoons lemon juice, 1 tablespoon chopped parsley, a pinch of grated nutmeg, and plenty of salt and pepper. Serve with long-grain rice.

 Hot-and-Sour Chicken Salad

Serves 4

2 cups coarsely chopped cooked chicken

1 (5 oz) package salad greens

1¾ cup thinly sliced button mushrooms

1 red chile, seeded and finely chopped

1 small bunch of cilantro leaves, stripped and chopped

1 tablespoon tom yum paste or Thai red curry paste

¼ cup vegetable oil

2 tablespoons lime juice

2 tablespoons coarsely chopped, roasted, salted cashew nuts (optional)

- Toss the chicken in a large bowl with the salad greens, mushrooms, chopped chile, and cilantro, then divide among 4 plates.

- Place the tom yum paste, vegetable oil, and lime juice in a jar with a tight-fitting lid, and shake until thoroughly combined. Drizzle over the salad, sprinkle with the cashew nuts, if using, and serve immediately.

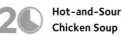

Hot-and-Sour Chicken Soup

Heat 2 cups chicken stock or water in a large saucepan with ¹/₃ cup tom yum paste and bring to a boil. Add 8 oz sliced, uncooked chicken breasts, then reduce the heat and simmer for 7–8 minutes, until the chicken is cooked. Stir in 1 cup coconut milk and 1¾ cups thinly sliced button mushrooms, then simmer for 1–2 minutes, until the mushrooms are just tender. Ladle into deep bowls, then squeeze over the lime juice and serve garnished with the chopped cilantro leaves and chile, if desired.

Hot-and-Sour Baked Chicken

Cut 3–4 slashes into each of 4 chicken breasts and rub all over with 3 tablespoons tom yum or Thai red curry paste. Finely chop the stalks from a small bunch of cilantro and mix with 1 lb sliced mushrooms. Spread them over the bottom of a large, foil-lined roasting pan and top with the chicken breasts. Drizzle 1 cup coconut milk over the chicken, then cover tightly with a large sheet of foil. Cook in a preheated oven, at 425°F, for 20–25 minutes, until cooked through. Squeeze over the lime juice and serve with 2¾ cups rice, steamed and garnished with the chopped cilantro leaves and chile, if desired.

30 Patatas Bravas

Serves 4

6 waxy potatoes (about 1½ lb),
    such as russets, peeled and cut
    into bite-size pieces
⅓ cup olive oil or vegetable oil
1 large onion, sliced
2 garlic cloves, crushed
½ teaspoon cayenne pepper
    or hot chili powder
½ teaspoon hot smoked paprika
2 cups tomato puree
2 tablespoons sherry vinegar
pinch of sugar
salt and pepper
2 tablespoons chopped parsley,
    to garnish (optional)

- Cook the potatoes in a large saucepan of lightly salted boiling water for 10 minutes, until just tender.

- Meanwhile, make the tomato sauce. Heat 2 tablespoons of the oil in a deep skillet and cook the onion for 4–5 minutes, then add the garlic and cook for an additional 2–3 minutes, until softened. Add the cayenne pepper and paprika and cook for 1 minute, then pour in the tomato puree, sherry vinegar, sugar, and plenty of salt and pepper. Bring to a boil, then reduce the heat and simmer gently for 15–20 minutes, until thickened, adding a splash of water if the sauce becomes too dry.

- Drain the potatoes thoroughly. Heat the remaining oil in a large nonstick skillet. Sauté the potatoes over medium heat for 15–20 minutes, turning occasionally, until crisp and golden, then stir in the tomato sauce, making sure the potatoes are coated thoroughly.

- Divide the patatas bravas among 4 shallow bowls. Sprinkle with the chopped parsley, if using, and serve immediately.

---

1 **Patatas Gnocchi Bravas** Heat the oil in a large skillet and sauté 1 (16 oz) package fresh gnocchi for 4–5 minutes, until crisp and golden. Meanwhile, chop 4 large tomatoes, place in a bowl with ½ teaspoon hot smoked paprika and 2 tablespoons sherry vinegar, and season. Remove the gnocchi with a slotted spoon and keep warm. Add the tomatoes to the skillet and stir for 2–3 minutes, until they begin to soften. Spoon into shallow bowls, top with the gnocchi, and serve immediately.

 Healthy Patatas Bravas Heat 2 teaspoons oil in a deep skillet and cook 2 garlic cloves, chopped, for 1–2 minutes, until softened. Add ½ teaspoon cayenne pepper or hot chili powder and ½ teaspoon hot smoked paprika, and cook for an additional 30–60 seconds, then stir in 2 cups tomato puree, 2 tablespoons sherry vinegar, and a pinch of sugar, and simmer gently for 15–18 minutes, until thickened. Meanwhile, cook 1½ lb small new potatoes in a saucepan of lightly salted boiling water for 12–15 minutes, until tender. Serve the potatoes with the spicy tomato sauce.

Meze Plate

Serves 4

butter, for greasing
1 egg
1 tablespoon milk
1 sheet store-bought puff pastry
3 tablespoons grated
  Parmesan-style cheese
7 oz feta cheese
⅓ cup olive oil
1 teaspoon dried oregano
1 (15 oz) can chickpeas, drained
  and rinsed
2 tablespoons lemon juice
1 teaspoon ground cumin
1 garlic clove, crushed
3–4 tablespoons plain yogurt
salt and pepper
¾ cup mixed olives

- Preheat the oven to 400°F and lightly grease a baking sheet. Beat the egg in a small bowl with the milk. Roll out the puff pastry sheet on a clean surface and brush with the beaten egg mixture. Sprinkle the grated cheese over the pastry, then fold the pastry in half lengthwise and press lightly. Cut into ½-inch strips and twist slightly. Place on the prepared baking sheet and cook in the preheated oven for 12–15 minutes, until crisp and golden.

- Meanwhile, cut the feta into thick slices and arrange on a plate. Drizzle with 1 tablespoon of the olive oil and sprinkle with the oregano and a pinch of black pepper. Set aside.

- To make a hummus, place all but 2 tablespoons of the chickpeas in a food processor with 3 tablespoons of the olive oil, the lemon juice, cumin, and garlic, and pulse to combine. Add enough yogurt to blend to a smooth, thick paste, then season and scrape into a bowl. Sprinkle with the reserved chickpeas and drizzle with the remaining olive oil.

- Remove the cheesy puff pastries from the oven and serve with the sliced feta, homemade hummus, and a bowl of mixed olives.

Meze-Style Nibbles

Heat a griddle pan until hot and toast 8 small flour tortillas for 30–60 seconds, turning once, until crisp and lightly charred. Cut into wedges and serve with 7 oz sliced feta cheese, ¾ cup mixed olives, and 1 cup each of store-bought hummus and taramasalata.

Meze-Style Tart

Cut 1 sheet store-bought puff pastry into quarters to make 4 rectangles, and place on a lightly greased baking sheet. Sprinkle with 1 cup baby spinach, leaving a border of about ½ inch, then fold up the border to make raised edges. Toss 1 cup drained and rinsed chickpeas in a bowl with 1 crushed garlic clove, 1 teaspoon ground cumin, and 1 tablespoon olive oil, then season lightly and spread the mixture over the spinach. Sprinkle with ⅔ cup crumbled feta cheese and brush the pastry edges with a little beaten egg. Cook in a preheated oven, at 350°F, for about 20 minutes, until crisp and golden. Serve with ¾ cup mixed olives.

30 Stilton, Potato, and Leek Soup

Serves 4

4 tablespoons butter

2 leeks, chopped

2 garlic cloves, finely chopped

6 floury potatoes (about 1½ lb), such as Yukon golds or white rounders, peeled and diced

6½ cups hot vegetable stock or chicken stock

⅔ cup crumbled Stilton or other strong blue cheese

½ cup light cream

salt and pepper

1 tablespoon chopped chives, to garnish

- Melt the butter in a large, heavy saucepan or casserole, and cook the leeks and garlic gently for 5 minutes, until soft and lightly golden. Add the potatoes and cook for an additional 1–2 minutes, then pour in the hot stock.

- Bring to a boil, then reduce the heat and simmer for 15–20 minutes, until the potatoes are really tender. Use a handheld immersion blender to blend until smooth.

- Add the Stilton and cream, and stir until melted, then season to taste and ladle into 4 deep bowls. Sprinkle with the chives and serve immediately with crusty bread.

---

1 **Stilton and Potato Gratin** Pour 1 cup light cream into a saucepan with 2 finely chopped garlic cloves, ⅔ cup crumbled Stilton or other strong blue cheese, 1 tablespoon chopped chives, 2 sliced scallions, and plenty of black pepper. Cook over medium heat for 1–2 minutes, until the cheese has melted. Meanwhile, arrange 12 store-bought hash browns in a large, shallow ovenproof dish, overlapping slightly. Pour over the hot cream mixture and cook under a preheated broiler for 6–7 minutes, until golden and bubbling. Serve with crusty bread and salad greens.

2 **Stilton and Gnocchi Casserole** Melt 4 tablespoons butter in a large, heavy saucepan or casserole, and cook 2 chopped leeks and 2 finely chopped garlic cloves gently for 5 minutes, until soft and lightly golden, then pour in 1 cup light cream, 1 tablespoon chopped chives, and plenty of black pepper. Meanwhile, cook 1 (16 oz) package gnocchi in a large saucepan of lightly salted boiling water according to the package directions, then drain and transfer to a shallow casserole. Pour over the hot leek and cream mixture, add ⅔ cup crumbled Stilton or other strong blue cheese over the top, and place in a preheated oven, at 450°F, for 12–15 minutes, until golden and bubbling.

10 Buttery Shrimp on Toast

Serves 4

4 slices of whole-grain bread
  or seeded bread
1 stick butter
pinch of cayenne pepper
10 oz shrimp, peeled
1 tablespoon lemon juice
2 tablespoons chopped chives
salt and pepper

- Toast the bread until golden and crisp.

- Place a large skillet over medium heat and melt the butter with the cayenne pepper. Once the butter begins to froth slightly, add the shrimp and cook for 2–3 minutes, stirring occasionally, until they are pink and cooked through.

- Add the lemon juice, then stir in the chives and season to taste. Spoon the shrimp and their buttery juices onto the hot toast and serve immediately.

2 Buttery Shrimp Spaghetti

Cook 1 lb spaghetti in a large saucepan of lightly salted boiling water for 8–10 minutes, or according to package directions, until tender but still firm to the bite. Meanwhile, cook 10 oz peeled shrimp in 1 stick butter and a pinch of cayenne pepper as above. Stir in 1 tablespoon lemon juice and 2 tablespoons chopped chives, then season. Drain the pasta, return to the pan, and add the shrimp and their juices. Stir to combine, then add 3 cups arugula and toss briefly before heaping into 4 shallow bowls. Serve with lemon wedges and cracked black pepper.

3 Buttery Baked Shrimp with Rice

Melt 4 tablespoons butter with 2 tablespoons olive oil or vegetable oil in a large, deep ovenproof skillet. Add 1 minced onion and cook for 5 minutes, until lightly golden. Stir in 2 finely chopped garlic cloves and ½ teaspoon each of ground nutmeg and cayenne pepper. Cook for an additional minute, then add 1 cup long-grain rice, and stir for 1 minute. Stir in 2 cups hot vegetable stock or fish stock, then season generously and cover with a lid. Place in a preheated oven, at 400°F, for about 15 minutes, until the rice is tender and the liquid has been absorbed. Sprinkle 10 oz peeled shrimp and 2 tablespoons chopped chives over the rice, then drizzle with 1 tablespoon lemon juice and 2 tablespoons melted butter. Cover and return to the oven for an additional 3–5 minutes, until the shrimp are just cooked. Spoon into 4 bowls and serve with lemon wedges, if desired.

Ham and Pea Soup with Crispy Bacon

Serves 4

2 tablespoons olive oil
   or vegetable oil
1 large onion, chopped
1 large potato (about 8 oz), such
   as Yukon gold or white rounder,
   peeled and diced
2 garlic cloves, chopped
2 cups frozen peas
4 cups hot ham stock or
   vegetable stock
2 cups chopped cooked ham
8 slices bacon
freshly ground black pepper
crusty white bread, to serve

- Heat the oil in a large, heavy saucepan or casserole and add the onion, potato, and garlic. Cook gently for 6–7 minutes, until softened.

- Add the peas, stock, and ham, and season generously with black pepper. Bring to a boil, then reduce the heat and simmer gently for about 10 minutes, until the potato is tender.

- Meanwhile, place the bacon slices on a foil-lined broiler pan and cook under a preheated broiler for 5–6 minutes, turning occasionally, until crispy and golden. Chop or crumble the broiled bacon into small pieces. Drain on paper towels.

- Use a handheld immersion blender to blend the soup until smooth and ladle into 4 bowls. Top with the crispy bacon and serve immediately, accompanied by crusty white bread.

Pea and Lentil Soup Drain 1 (15 oz) can lentils in water and place in a medium saucepan with 2 cups frozen peas, 2 cups chopped cooked ham, and 4 cups hot ham stock or vegetable stock. Bring to a boil, season with black pepper, and simmer gently for 5–6 minutes. Meanwhile, cook 8 bacon slices following the main recipe. Blend the soup until smooth, ladle into 4 bowls, and serve topped with the crispy bacon.

Pea and Ham Risotto Melt 2 tablespoons butter with 1 tablespoon olive oil and cook 1 large chopped onion and 2 chopped garlic cloves for 6–7 minutes, until softened. Add 2 cups risotto rice and stir for 1–2 minutes, until the grains are translucent. Stir in 1 cup dry white wine and cook until it has been absorbed, then add 4¼ cups boiling ham stock or vegetable stock, a small ladleful at a time, stirring frequently until all the liquid has been absorbed and the rice is just tender. This should take 17–18 minutes. About 2 minutes before the end of the cooking time, stir 2 cups frozen peas and 2 cups chopped cooked ham into the risotto. Meanwhile, cook 8 bacon slices following the main recipe. Serve the risotto spooned into bowls, topped with the crispy bacon.

BUD-SOUP-SAA

30 Chicken Noodle Broth

Serves 4

4 skinless chicken thighs
(about 1 lb in total)
5 cups chicken stock
or vegetable stock
2 tablespoons vegetable oil
1 red bell pepper, cored, seeded,
and sliced
4 scallions, cut into ¾-inch
lengths
1 tablespoon chopped fresh
ginger root
3 cups sliced button mushrooms
8 oz medium dried egg noodles
1–2 tablespoons dark soy sauce
2 tablespoons chopped fresh
cilantro

- Place the chicken thighs in a saucepan and pour the stock over them. Bring to a boil, reduce the heat, and simmer gently for 20 minutes, until the chicken is cooked through.

- Meanwhile, heat the oil in a large saucepan or wok, add the red bell pepper and scallions, and cook for 4–5 minutes. Add the ginger and mushrooms and cook gently for an additional 4–5 minutes, until softened and golden.

- Use a slotted spoon to remove the chicken from the stock and set aside to cool slightly. Add the noodles to the stock, turn off the heat, cover, and set aside for 4–5 minutes, or according to package directions, until just tender. Add the cooked vegetables and season with the soy sauce.

- Once the chicken thighs are cool enough to handle, remove and discard the bones, then shred the meat and return to the soup. Ladle the soup and noodles into 4 large bowls. Sprinkle with the chopped cilantro and serve immediately.

---

1 **Chicken Noodle Salad** Cook 8 oz medium dried egg noodles according to package directions. Cool under cold running water. Meanwhile, slice 1 red bell pepper, 4 scallions, and 7 oz button mushrooms (about 3 cups). Combine ¼ cup vegetable oil, 2 teaspoons sesame oil (if using), 2 tablespoons light soy sauce, and 2 teaspoons minced ginger (from a jar). Toss the cooled noodles with the vegetables and dressing, and serve immediately, sprinkled with 2 tablespoons chopped fresh cilantro, if desired.

2 **Chicken, Noodle, and Broccoli Broth** Thinly slice 4 skinless, boneless chicken thighs. Heat 2 tablespoons vegetable oil in a large saucepan or wok, add 4 scallions, cut into ¾-inch lengths, and 2 cups small broccoli florets, and cook for 4–5 minutes. Add the sliced chicken and 1 tablespoon chopped fresh ginger root and cook for 4–5 minutes, until the chicken is cooked and golden. Add 5 cups chicken stock or vegetable stock, bring to a boil, and season to taste with 1–2 tablespoons dark soy sauce. Cook 8 oz straight-to-wok rice noodles according to package directions, and divide among 4 deep, warm bowls. Ladle the soup on top and sprinkle with chopped cilantro, if desired.

BUD-SOUP-ROQ

Giant Tomato and Rosemary Muffins

Serves 4

3 tablespoons peanut oil,
   plus extra for greasing
2 tablespoons grated Parmesan-
   style cheese
1⅔ cups whole-wheat flour
1 teaspoon baking powder
¾ teaspoon baking soda
¼ teaspoon black pepper
1 teaspoon dried rosemary
½ teaspoon ground onion powder
¼ teaspoon ground garlic powder
⅓ cup chopped sun-dried
   tomatoes
1 cup whole-milk plain yogurt
2 extra-large eggs, beaten
2 tablespoons tomato paste

- Preheat the oven to 400°F and grease a 6-cup muffin pan with cups approximately 3½ inches across and 2 inches deep.

- Mix half of the cheese in a large bowl with the flour, baking powder, baking soda, black pepper, rosemary, and onion and garlic powder. Mix half of the sun-dried tomatoes with the yogurt, eggs, and tomato paste in another bowl. Pour the wet ingredients into the dry ingredients and stir with a large spoon until just combined.

- Divide the batter among the cups in the pan, then top with the remaining sun-dried tomatoes and grated cheese. Bake in the preheated oven for 18–20 minutes, or until a toothpick inserted into one of the muffins comes out clean. Cool for a few minutes on a wire rack, then serve.

 Toasted Tomato and Rosemary Muffins Slice 4 English, oven-bottom muffins in half and lay, cut side up, on a baking sheet. Spread each half with 2 tablespoons tomato paste and sprinkle with 1 teaspoon dried rosemary and 3 tablespoons grated cheese. Cook under a preheated broiler for 3–4 minutes. Meanwhile, slice 3 tomatoes and 4 oz mozzarella cheese, arrange on 4 plates, and drizzle with a little peanut oil. Place the muffins on the plates and serve drizzled with balsamic vinegar, if desired.

Tomato, Rosemary and Garlic Pizza Bread Place ⅓ cup chopped sun-dried tomatoes and 2 tablespoons tomato paste in a mini chopper or the small bowl of a food processor with 1 large crushed garlic clove and 1 stick slightly softened butter. Blend until smooth, then stir in 1 teaspoon dried rosemary and 2 tablespoons grated Parmesan-style cheese. Spread the paste over 2 store-bought pizza crusts, approximately 10 inches in diameter, and place on 1 or 2 baking sheets. Cook in a preheated oven, at 350°F, for 10–12 minutes, until melted and lightly golden. Serve in wedges as an appetizer or snack.

Chorizo and Roasted Red Pepper Tortilla

Serves 4

2 tablespoons olive oil
8 oz chorizo, diced
1 large red onion, halved and sliced
2 garlic cloves, chopped
1 teaspoon hot smoked paprika
½ teaspoon dried thyme
1 teaspoon dried oregano
1 (12 oz) jar roasted red peppers, drained, rinsed, and cut into strips
6 eggs, lightly beaten
2 tablespoons chopped flat leaf parsley
1 cup shredded cheddar cheese
freshly ground black pepper

- Heat the oil in a large nonstick skillet and add the chorizo and onion. Cook gently for 2–3 minutes, then stir in the garlic. Cook for 4–5 minutes, until softened. Stir in the spices and dried herbs and cook for an additional 2 minutes, then add the roasted peppers.

- Beat the eggs with the parsley and season with black pepper. Pour the egg mixture into the skillet and cook gently for 3–4 minutes, stirring occasionally to prevent the bottom from burning, until the egg is almost set.

- Sprinkle with the shredded cheddar, then slide under a preheated hot broiler, keeping the handle away from the heat. Broil for 2–3 minutes, until golden and set. Slice into wedges and serve immediately.

 Chorizo and Roasted Red Pepper Bagels Slice 4 bagels in half and toast until lightly golden. Place, cut side up, on a baking sheet and top with 3 oz thinly sliced chorizo, 1 (7 oz) jar roasted red peppers, drained and sliced, 1 cup shredded cheddar cheese, and 1 teaspoon dried oregano. Cook under a preheated broiler for 4–5 minutes, until bubbling. Meanwhile, heat 1 tablespoon of olive oil in a skillet until hot and break 4 medium eggs into the skillet. Cook for 2–3 minutes, until the white is set but the yolk is still runny. Arrange the bagels on 4 plates and top each with a fried egg and a sprinkle of black pepper.

Baked Eggs with Chorizo and Roasted Red Peppers Heat 2 tablespoons olive oil in a large, ovenproof skillet and add 8 oz diced chorizo and 1 large red onion, halved and thinly sliced. Cook gently for 2–3 minutes, then stir in 2 chopped garlic cloves. Cook for 4–5 minutes, until softened. Stir in 1 teaspoon each of hot smoked paprika and dried oregano, ½ teaspoon dried thyme, 1 (12 oz) jar roasted red peppers, drained and rinsed, and 4 diced, large ripe tomatoes. Cook gently for 7–8 minutes, until the tomatoes have softened. Divide the tomato mixture among 4 individual ovenproof dishes, then crack an egg into the center of each one. Season with black pepper and cook in a preheated oven, at 400°F, for 8–10 minutes, or until the egg white is set but the yolk is still slightly runny. Serve with crusty bread.

30 Tandoori Chicken Wings with Raita

Serves 4

2 tablespoons tandoori paste

1 teaspoon cumin seeds

¼ cup plain yogurt

2 teaspoons lemon juice

8–12 chicken wings (about 1½ lb in total)

For the raita

1 medium cucumber

1 cup plain yogurt

2 teaspoons lemon juice

½ teaspoon ground cumin

salt and pepper

To serve

½ iceberg lettuce, shredded

4–8 poppadoms (optional)

- Preheat the oven to 425°F and line a baking sheet with foil. Mix the tandoori paste, cumin seeds, yogurt, and lemon juice in a large, shallow dish. Make 2–3 shallow cuts in each chicken wing and place in the dish. Use your fingers to coat the chicken wings thoroughly with the tandoori yogurt.

- Arrange the wings in a single layer on the prepared baking sheet and cook in the preheated oven for 20–25 minutes, until slightly charred and the juices run clear when the thickest part of the chicken is pierced with the tip of a sharp knife.

- In the meantime, make the raita. Halve the cucumber lengthwise and use a spoon to remove the seeds. Coarsely grate the flesh and place in the middle of a clean dish towel, then bring up the edges and twist the cucumber in the dish towel over a sink to squeeze out the excess moisture. Place the cucumber in a bowl, add the yogurt, lemon juice, and ground cumin, then season with salt and pepper and chill until the chicken is cooked.

- Serve the cooked chicken wings with the shredded lettuce, cool raita, and crisp poppadoms, if using.

 Tandoori Chicken Pitas

Mix 1 tablespoon tandoori paste in a bowl with ⅔ cup plain yogurt, 1 tablespoon chopped mint, ½ teaspoon ground cumin, 2 teaspoons lemon juice, and plenty of salt and pepper. Fold in 2 cups diced, cooked chicken and stir thoroughly to coat, then spoon into 4 large, warm whole-wheat pita breads. Add some shredded lettuce and serve immediately.

Broiled Tandoori Chicken with Raita

Place 4 chicken breasts (about 1¼ lb in total), one at a time, between 2 large pieces of plastic wrap and beat with a rolling pin to flatten slightly. Mix 2 tablespoons tandoori paste with ¼ cup plain yogurt and rub all over the chicken breasts. Set aside to marinate for 8–10 minutes. Meanwhile, prepare the raita following the main recipe. Place the chicken breasts on a foil-lined broiler rack and cook under a preheated broiler for 7–8 minutes, turning once, until cooked through. Remove from the broiler, slice thickly, and serve with ½ shredded iceberg lettuce, the raita, and 4–8 crisp poppadoms, if desired.

BUD-SOUP-GON

Creamy Baked Eggs with Blue Cheese

Serves 4

butter, for greasing and spreading
3 oz blue cheese, such as Stilton, Roquefort, or Gorgonzola
⅔ cup heavy cream
2 tablespoons chopped chives
½ teaspoon cracked black pepper
4 extra-large eggs
4 slices of whole-grain bread

- Preheat the oven to 400°F and butter 4 ramekins. In a small bowl, mash the blue cheese into the cream using the back of a fork. Stir in the chives and black pepper and divide among the ramekins.

- Crack an egg into each ramekin and place them in a roasting pan. Pour hot water into the pan so that it comes about halfway up the sides of the ramekins. Cook in the preheated oven for 7–8 minutes, or until the egg white is set but the yolk is still runny.

- Meanwhile, toast the bread until golden and butter lightly. Cut into strips for dipping, if desired. Remove the baked eggs from the oven and serve immediately with the toast.

 Creamy Scrambled Eggs with Blue Cheese Beat 8 eggs in a bowl with ¼ cup whole milk and plenty of black pepper. Melt 1 tablespoon butter in a large nonstick saucepan until frothy, then pour in the eggs. Once the eggs begin to set, use a heat-resistant rubber spatula to fold gently over low heat for 5–6 minutes, until the eggs are creamy and lightly set. Remove from the heat and sprinkle with ½ cup crumbled blue cheese and 2 tablespoons chopped chives. Serve the eggs spooned over 4 slices of hot, buttered toast.

 Creamy Blue Cheese and Egg Pie Grease a shallow pie plate, approximately 9 inches across and 1 inch deep, and line with 1 sheet store-bought, rolled pie crust dough. Squeeze the excess moisture from 1 (10 oz) package defrosted spinach and place in a bowl with ½ cup heavy cream, 2 tablespoons chives, 4 extra-large eggs, and plenty of black pepper. Stir to just combine, then pour the mixture into the pie crust shell. Cover with a second sheet of rolled piecrust dough and squeeze together the edges to seal, trimming off any excess dough. Brush with beaten egg and cut 2 little slits in the center of the pie. Cook in a preheated oven, at 400°F, for about 22 minutes, until the pastry is crisp and golden.

30 Lemon and Spinach Soup with White Rice

Serves 4

2 tablespoons olive oil
  or vegetable oil
1 large onion, finely chopped
2 garlic cloves, finely chopped
1 cup long-grain
  white rice, rinsed
5 cups clear chicken stock
¼ cup lemon juice
3 extra-large eggs, beaten
4 cups rinsed, trimmed, and
  chopped spinach
salt and pepper

To serve

2 tablespoons chopped parsley
2 tablespoons grated Parmesan-
  style cheese

- Heat the oil in a large saucepan or casserole and cook the onion and garlic gently for 7–8 minutes, until softened. Stir in the rice and cook for 1 minute, then pour in the chicken stock. Simmer gently for 12–15 minutes, until the rice is just tender. Remove from the heat.

- In a small bowl, whisk the lemon juice with the beaten eggs and a pinch of salt. Continue whisking while you add a ladleful of hot stock in a slow, steady stream, then whisk the egg mixture into the saucepan of soup. Return the pan to low heat and continue stirring for 2–3 minutes, until the soup has thickened slightly, being careful not to let it boil.

- Stir in the chopped spinach and season to taste, then ladle the soup into 4 bowls. Serve sprinkled with chopped parsley and grated cheese.

 Quick Lemon and Spinach Soup

Heat 4 cups chicken stock to boiling point in a large saucepan. Add 3 cups cooked rice, stir until heated through, then remove from the heat. In a small bowl, whisk ¼ cup lemon juice with 3 extra-large eggs and a pinch of salt. Continue whisking while you add a ladleful of hot stock in a slow, steady stream, then whisk the egg mixture into the saucepan of soup to thicken. Stir in 4 cups rinsed, trimmed, and chopped spinach and serve.

 Creamy Lemon and Chicken Rice

Heat 2 tablespoons olive oil or vegetable oil in a large, deep skillet and cook 2¾ cups diced chicken breast or thigh over medium-high heat for 6–7 minutes, until golden. Reduce the heat, add 1 large onion, finely chopped, and 2 garlic cloves, finely chopped, and cook for 4–5 minutes, until softened and lightly golden. Stir in ¼ cup lemon juice and ½ cup hot chicken stock and simmer gently for 2–3 minutes, until the chicken is just cooked through.

Pour 1¼ cups heavy cream into the skillet, then season to taste. Stir in 4 cups rinsed, trimmed, and chopped spinach and heat until just wilted. Serve immediately with 3 cups cooked rice.

10 Cauliflower Coleslaw Pockets

Serves 4

½ small cauliflower, cut into small florets
1 carrot, peeled and shredded
1 celery stick, thinly sliced
2 scallions, thinly sliced
¼ cup mayonnaise
1 teaspoon chipotle paste or sun-dried tomato paste
1 tablespoon red wine vinegar
½ teaspoon sugar
salt and pepper
4 large, whole-wheat pita breads, warmed, to serve

- Combine the cauliflower, carrot, celery, and scallion in a large bowl. In a separate bowl, mix together the mayonnaise, chipotle paste, vinegar, and sugar, and season with salt and pepper.

- Add the dressing to the vegetables and mix until really well coated. Spoon the mixture into the pita breads and serve immediately.

 Pan-Roasted Cauliflower and Chickpea Salad Heat 2 tablespoons oil in a skillet. Add 2 scallions, thinly sliced, and cook for 1 minute, until just softened. Add ¼ small cauliflower, cut into small florets, then chop 1 celery stick and 1 peeled carrot and add to the skillet with 1 teaspoon chipotle paste or 2 tablespoons tomato paste. Cook for 1–2 minutes before adding 1 tablespoon red vinegar and ¾ cup vegetable stock. Cover and simmer gently for 5–6 minutes, until just tender but still with some bite. Add 1 (15 oz) can chickpeas, drained, and cook for 1–2 minutes, stirring occasionally. Spoon into bowls and serve with warm pita breads.

 Spicy Roast Cauliflower Place ½ small cauliflower, cut into small florets, in a large bowl, then cut 1 peeled carrot, 1 celery stick, and 2 scallions into bite-size pieces. Toss with 2 tablespoons olive oil or vegetable oil, 1 teaspoon chipotle or tomato paste, 1 tablespoon red wine vinegar, and 1 teaspoon honey. Season and transfer to a large roasting pan. Cook in a preheated oven, at 400°F, for 20–25 minutes, until just tender and golden but still with some bite. For a more substantial meal, toss with 2 cups cooked couscous and serve with warm pita breads and ¼ cup plain yogurt.

 # Tofu Ramen Noodle Soup

Serves 4

1 oz dried whole shiitake
mushrooms

5 cups vegetable stock

1–2 tablespoons light soy sauce,
plus extra to serve

8 oz dried ramen or egg noodles

12 oz firm tofu, sliced

2 cups bean sprouts

2 scallions, finely sliced

- Place the mushrooms in a saucepan with the vegetable stock, cover, bring to a boil, then simmer gently for about 15 minutes, until softened. Remove with a slotted spoon, cool slightly, then slice the fleshy parts thickly and return to the pan, discarding the tough stems. Season the soup with soy sauce.

- Meanwhile, bring a large saucepan of water to a boil, add the noodles, and immediately remove from the heat. Cover and set aside for 4–5 minutes, until tender. Alternatively, cook according to the package directions. Mound the noodles into 4 warm bowls.

- Top the noodles with the slices of tofu and bean sprouts, then ladle the hot mushrooms and broth over them. Sprinkle with the scallions and serve immediately, with extra soy sauce, if desired.

Mushroom Noodle Stir-Fry

Heat 2 tablespoons vegetable oil in a large skillet or wok, add 1 tablespoon chopped fresh ginger root and 2 chopped garlic cloves, and cook for 1–2 minutes, until softened. Add 5 cups sliced button mushrooms and stir-fry for 3–4 minutes, until almost tender. Stir in 1 (11 oz) jar prepared Chinese stir-fry sauce and heat until just simmering. Spoon the mushroom mixture over 1 lb egg noodles, cooked, and serve immediately.

Vegetable Noodle Soup

Simmer 1 oz dried whole shiitake mushrooms in 3 cups hot vegetable stock in a saucepan, following the main recipe, then slice as above and set aside. Heat 2 tablespoons vegetable oil in a skillet or wok, and stir-fry 2 scallions, finely sliced, with 1 tablespoon chopped fresh ginger root and 2 chopped garlic cloves for 1–2 minutes, until softened. Add the sliced shiitake mushrooms to the pan and stir-fry for 2–3 minutes, then add 2 cups bean sprouts and 1 cup thinly sliced snow peas and cook for an additional 1–2 minutes. Add 1½ cups of the hot mushroom stock to the pan and season with 1–2 tablespoons light soy sauce. Add 10 oz straight-to-wok udon or egg noodles, cook until hot, then mound into bowls and spoon the soupy broth over the noodles and vegetables. Serve topped with 12 oz firm tofu, sliced, if desired.

BUD-SOUP-CYD

30 Zucchini and Bacon Carbonara Frittata

Serves 4

8 oz spaghetti
2 tablespoons butter
1 tablespoon olive or vegetable oil
5 oz smoked bacon, chopped
1 medium zucchini, shredded
2 garlic cloves, chopped
4 extra-large eggs, lightly beaten
½ cup light cream
½ cup grated Parmesan-style
   cheese
salt and pepper

- Cook the spaghetti according to the package directions. Meanwhile, melt the butter with the oil in a large, nonstick skillet and add the bacon. Cook for 4–5 minutes, until golden.

- Place the zucchini in the middle of a clean dish towel, bring up the edges, and twist the towel over a sink to squeeze out the excess moisture. Add to the bacon with the garlic and cook for an additional 4–5 minutes, until soft and golden. Meanwhile, mix the beaten eggs in a small bowl with the cream, half the cheese, and plenty of seasoning.

- Transfer the zucchini and bacon to a large bowl, then toss with the drained pasta and egg mixture. Return to the skillet and cook over medium-low heat for 5–6 minutes. Sprinkle with the remaining cheese, then slide under a preheated hot broiler, keeping the handle away from the heat. Broil for 4–5 minutes, until golden and set. Slice into wedges and serve immediately.

 Zucchini and Bacon Carbonara

Heat 2 tablespoons butter and 1 tablespoon oil in a skillet and cook 5 oz chopped smoked bacon for 3–4 minutes. Meanwhile, cook 1 lb thin spaghetti according to the package directions. Prepare 1 medium zucchini, shredded, as above, add to the bacon with 2 chopped garlic cloves, and cook for 3–4 minutes. Meanwhile, beat 2 egg yolks and 2 eggs in a bowl with 1¼ cups light cream, ½ cup grated Parmesan-style cheese, and black pepper. Return the drained pasta to the pan and toss with the zucchini, bacon, and egg mixture.

 Zucchini and Bacon Carbonara Gratin

Cook 10 oz pasta shapes in a large saucepan of lightly salted boiling water according to the package directions until al dente. Meanwhile, cook 5 oz smoked bacon, chopped, 1 medium zucchini, shredded, and 2 garlic cloves, chopped, following the main recipe. Beat 2 egg yolks and 2 eggs in a bowl with 1¼ cups light cream, ½ cup grated Parmesan-style cheese, and plenty of black pepper. Drain the pasta, return to the pan, and toss with the zucchini, bacon, and egg mixture, until well coated. Transfer to a large, shallow ovenproof dish and sprinkle with an additional ½ cup grated cheese. Cook under a preheated broiler for 7–8 minutes, until the cheesy topping is golden. Serve with a green salad.

 # Roasted Chickpeas with Spinach

Serves 4

1 (15 oz) can chickpeas, drained
  and rinsed
3 tablespoons olive oil
  or vegetable oil
1 teaspoon cumin seeds
1 teaspoon paprika
½ red onion, thinly sliced
3 ripe tomatoes, coarsely
  chopped
3½ cups young spinach leaves
2 tablespoons lemon juice
4 oz feta cheese (optional)
lemon wedges, to garnish
salt and pepper

· Preheat the oven to 425°F. Mix the chickpeas in a bowl with 1 tablespoon oil, the cumin seeds, and the paprika and season with salt and pepper. Transfer to a large nonstick roasting pan and roast in the preheated oven for 12–15 minutes, until nutty and golden.

· Meanwhile, place the onion and tomatoes in a large bowl with the spinach and toss gently to combine. Mound onto 4 serving plates.

· Remove the chickpeas from the oven and sprinkle them over the spinach salad. Crumble the feta over the top, if using, and drizzle each plate with the lemon juice and the remaining olive oil. Garnish with lemon wedges and serve immediately.

10 Chickpea and Spinach Salad

Toss 1 (15 oz) can chickpeas, drained and rinsed, with 3 tablespoons olive oil or vegetable oil and 1 teaspoon each of cumin seeds and paprika. Season with salt and pepper. Transfer to a large skillet and heat for 2–3 minutes, stirring occasionally, until hot and fragrant. Remove from the heat, toss with ½ red onion, thinly sliced, and 3 ripe tomatoes, coarsely chopped, and fold into 3½ cups torn young spinach. Mound onto serving plates and serve with ⅔ cup crumbled feta cheese, if desired.

30 Aromatic Chickpea and Spinach Stew

Heat 2 tablespoons olive oil or vegetable oil in a large, deep skillet or casserole. Chop 1 red onion, 2 large garlic cloves, and a ¾-inch piece of fresh ginger root. Add to the skillet and cook gently for about 10 minutes, until softened and lightly golden. Add 1 teaspoon each of cumin seeds and paprika and cook for an additional minute, then add 4 large, ripe, diced tomatoes, 1 (15 oz) can chickpeas, drained and rinsed, 2 tablespoons lemon juice, and ½ cup hot water or vegetable stock. Bring to a boil, reduce the heat, and simmer gently, covered, for 12–15 minutes, until softened and thickened. Season to taste, then stir in 3½ cups torn young spinach and cook gently until wilted. Spoon into 4 shallow bowls and serve sprinkled with 2 tablespoons chopped parsley and ⅔ cup crumbled feta cheese, if desired.

Staples Spicy Bean Soup

Serves 4

2 tablespoons vegetable oil

1 large onion, chopped

1 red bell pepper, cored, seeded, and chopped

2 garlic cloves, chopped

1 (1¼ oz) envelope Mexican fajita, taco, or chili con carne spice mix

1 (15 oz) can kidney beans, drained and rinsed

1 (15 oz) can black beans, drained and rinsed

1 (14½ oz) can tomatoes

3 cups boiling water

1 beef or vegetable bouillon cube

To serve

¼ cup sour cream

tortilla chips (optional)

- Heat the vegetable oil in a large, heavy saucepan or casserole and cook the onion and bell pepper over medium-high heat for 4 minutes. Add the garlic and sauté for an additional 2 minutes, until lightly colored.

- Stir in the spice mix, then add half of the beans, the chopped tomatoes, measured water, and bouillon cube. Stir well, bring to a boil, and simmer for 10–12 minutes, until slightly thickened.

- Use a handheld immersion blender to blend the soup until almost smooth, then stir in the remaining beans and heat through. Ladle into 4 deep bowls and serve immediately with a drizzle of sour cream and a sprinkling of tortilla chips, if desired.

Spicy Bean Tacos Heat 2 tablespoons oil in a large saucepan and cook 1 large onion, chopped, and 1 red bell pepper, cored, seeded, and chopped, for 4 minutes. Add 2 garlic cloves, chopped, and sauté for an additional 2 minutes. Add 1 (1¼ oz) envelope Mexican fajita, taco, or chili con carne spice mix, 1 (15 oz) can each of kidney beans and black beans, 2 diced tomatoes, and ¼ cup water. Simmer for 2–3 minutes, then spoon into 8 warm taco shells and serve immediately with ¼ cup sour cream.

Spicy Bean Enchiladas Follow the 10-minute recipe to make the spicy bean mixture, then divide it among 8 small, soft flour tortillas and sprinkle with ⅔ cup shredded cheddar cheese or mozzarella cheese. Tuck in the ends and roll each tortilla tightly, then place close together in a snug-fitting ovenproof dish. Pour 1 (10 oz) jar of hot Mexican salsa over the tortillas and sprinkle an additional ⅔ cup shredded cheese over the tortillas. Cook in a preheated oven, at 400°F, for about 15 minutes, until hot and bubbling. Serve with ¼ cup sour cream.

QuickCook
Veggie Delights

Recipes listed by cooking time

3⊙

2⊙

10

Creamy Mushroom and Tarragon Rigatoni

Serves 4

4 tablespoons butter

1 tablespoon olive oil
or vegetable oil

1 large leek, thinly sliced

1 garlic clove, chopped

2 cups sliced button mushrooms

1 teaspoon dried tarragon

1 lb rigatoni or tortiglioni pasta

½ cup dry white wine or
vegetable stock

1 cup light cream

salt and pepper

4 teaspoons grated Parmesan-
style cheese, to serve

- Heat the butter and oil in a large nonstick skillet until the butter is frothing. Add the leek and garlic and cook for 2–3 minutes, until beginning to soften. Add the mushrooms and tarragon and cook for an additional 4–5 minutes, until soft and golden.

- Meanwhile, cook the pasta in a large saucepan of lightly salted boiling water for 11 minutes, or according to the package directions, until al dente.

- Pour the white wine and cream into the mushrooms and season generously with salt and pepper. Simmer gently for 6–7 minutes.

- Drain the pasta and stir into the sauce. Spoon into 4 shallow bowls and serve immediately, sprinkled with grated Parmesan.

 Quick Creamy Mushroom Penne

Heat 4 tablespoons butter and 1 tablespoon oil in a large skillet. Add 1 thinly sliced large leek and 1 chopped garlic clove, and cook for 2–3 minutes. Add 2 cups sliced mushrooms and 1 tablespoon chopped fresh tarragon and cook for an additional 4–5 minutes. Cook 1 lb quick-cook or fresh penne pasta according to the package directions. Stir ⅔ cup cream cheese and 8 sliced sun-dried tomatoes into the mushrooms with 1 cup light cream, then bring to a boil and season. Pour the sauce over the drained pasta and serve with 4 teaspoons grated Parmesan-style cheese.

Creamy-Topped Mushroom Casserole Make the sauce following the 10-minute recipe, but use 1 teaspoon dried tarragon instead of the fresh tarragon. Cook 1 lb quick-cook penne pasta in a large saucepan of lightly salted boiling water and drain after 3 minutes. Meanwhile, beat 1 egg and 1 egg yolk with 4 teaspoons grated Parmesan-style cheese and 1¼ cup Greek yogurt, then season lightly and set aside. Stir the pasta into the mushroom sauce and then transfer to a large ovenproof dish. Top with the egg and yogurt mixture, then cook in a preheated oven, at 400°F, for about 20 minutes until bubbling and golden. Serve with crusty bread.

Zucchini, Garlic, and Chile Fusilli

Serves 4

1 lb quick-cook or prepared fresh fusilli pasta

2 medium zucchini, shredded

¼ cup olive oil or vegetable oil

1 red chile, finely chopped

2 garlic cloves, finely chopped

2 tablespoons lemon juice

3 tablespoons chopped flat leaf parsley (optional)

salt and pepper

½ cup grated Parmesan-style cheese, to serve (optional)

- Cook the pasta in a large saucepan of lightly salted boiling water for 4–5 minutes, or according to the package directions, until al dente.

- Meanwhile, place the zucchini in the middle of a clean dish towel, bring up the edges, and twist the zucchini in the towel over a sink to squeeze out the excess moisture.

- Heat the oil in a nonstick skillet with the chile and garlic and cook gently for 1 minute, until the oil is fragrant. Increase the heat slightly and add the zucchini. Cook gently for 5–6 minutes, until soft and golden.

- Drain the pasta and stir in the zucchini mixture, lemon juice, and parsley, if using. Season with salt and pepper, and serve immediately with the cheese, if using.

2 **Zucchini and Garlic Quick Risotto**

Heat ¼ cup olive oil or vegetable oil in a nonstick skillet with 1 finely chopped red chile and 2 finely chopped garlic cloves and cook gently for 1 minute, until the oil is fragrant. Increase the heat, add 2 medium zucchini, shredded, and sauté for 3–4 minutes, until just golden, then stir in 8 oz orzo (rice-shaped pasta). Alternatively, use small pasta shapes. Add 2 cups hot vegetable stock and plenty of seasoning and bring to a boil. Reduce the heat, cover with a lid, and cook for about 10 minutes, until the liquid has been absorbed and the pasta is tender. Use a fork to stir through 3 tablespoons chopped flat leaf parsley and 2 tablespoons lemon juice, then check the seasoning and serve with grated cheese, if desired.

 ### 3 **Crispy-Topped Zucchini and Garlic Casserole** Follow

the main recipe, but use only 2 tablespoons parsley. Stir 1 cup mascarpone into the pasta, season, and transfer to a large, ovenproof dish. Mix 1⅔ cups fresh bread crumbs with ½ cup grated Parmesan-style cheese and the remaining tablespoon of parsley, and sprinkle the mix over the pasta. Cook in a preheated oven, at 375°F, for 15–20 minutes, until bubbling and golden. Serve with a green salad, if desired.

30 Tomato, Bean, and New Potato Gratin

Serves 4

1½ lb small new potatoes

3 tablespoons olive oil
or vegetable oil

1 onion, chopped

1 celery stick, chopped

2 garlic cloves, chopped

3 tablespoons store-bought
pesto

4 medium ripe tomatoes, diced

⅔ cup hot vegetable stock
or water

1 (15 oz) can cranberry beans
or kidney beans, drained
and rinsed

1 cup fresh or defrosted green
beans (1-inch pieces)

½ cup grated Parmesan-style
cheese

salt and pepper

- Cook the new potatoes in a saucepan of lightly salted boiling water for about 10 minutes, until just tender. Drain and cool slightly, then cut into ¼-inch slices.

- Meanwhile, heat 2 tablespoons of oil in a large, deep skillet and cook the onion for 2 minutes. Add the celery and cook for an additional 2 minutes, then add the garlic and cook for a final 2–3 minutes, stirring frequently, until lightly golden.

- Stir the pesto into the onions, then add the diced tomatoes, stock, cranberry beans, and green beans. Season generously with salt and pepper and bring to a boil, reduce the heat, and simmer for 5 minutes, until the tomatoes soften and the beans are tender.

- Transfer the vegetable mixture to a large ovenproof dish, and arrange the sliced potatoes over the top. Sprinkle with the grated cheese, drizzle with the remaining oil, and cook under a preheated broiler for 7–8 minutes, until golden.

 Quick Tomato and Bean Salad Shred 2 carrots and thinly slice 2 celery sticks. Toss with 1 (15 oz) can cranberry beans or kidney beans, drained and rinsed, and 4 medium, diced tomatoes, then divide among 4 serving bowls. Mix 2 tablespoons store-bought pesto with 2 tablespoons oil and 1 tablespoon balsamic vinegar. Season and drizzle over the salad to serve.

Tomato and Lentil Curry Heat 2 tablespoons vegetable oil in a heavy casserole over medium-high heat, then sauté 1 chopped onion, 1 chopped celery stick, and 2 chopped garlic cloves for 5–6 minutes, until lightly browned. Stir in ¼ cup medium curry paste and cook gently for 2 minutes. Add 4 medium, diced tomatoes, 1 (15 oz) can lentils, drained (or 2 cups cooked lentils), and 1 cup hot water or vegetable stock, and simmer gently, uncovered, for about 10 minutes, until thickened and fragrant. Serve hot in shallow bowls with warm naan.

3 Sweet Potato and Coconut Rice

Serves 4

3 tablespoons vegetable oil

3 medium sweet potatoes
(about 1¼ lb), peeled and
cut into ¾-inch cubes

1-inch piece of fresh ginger root,
peeled and finely chopped

2 garlic cloves, thinly sliced

1 teaspoon cumin seeds

1 red chile, seeded and chopped
(optional)

1⅓ cups long-grain rice

1½ cups hot vegetable stock

1 cup coconut milk

2 tablespoons coconut shavings
or shredded dried coconut

salt and pepper

· Heat the oil in a large, nonstick saucepan or casserole with a tight-fitting lid. Add the sweet potato, ginger, garlic, cumin seeds, and chile, if using, and sauté gently for 5–6 minutes, until lightly golden.

· Add the rice and stir for a minute, until well coated. Pour in the hot stock and coconut milk and bring to a boil. Reduce the heat, season generously with salt and pepper, and cover with the lid. Simmer gently for 15–17 minutes, until the liquid has been absorbed and the rice and potatoes are tender.

· Meanwhile, toast the coconut in a dry skillet for 3–4 minutes, until golden. Transfer to a plate to cool.

· Fluff up the rice with a fork and spoon into shallow bowls. Sprinkle with the toasted coconut and serve immediately.

---

1 **Aromatic Coconut Rice** Heat 3 tablespoons vegetable oil in a large, nonstick skillet and sauté a 1-inch piece of fresh ginger root, peeled and finely chopped, 2 sliced garlic cloves, 1 teaspoon cumin seeds, and 1 seeded and chopped red chile, if using, for 2–3 minutes. Stir in 3 cups cooked rice and 1 cup coconut milk. Stir over medium heat for 2–3 minutes, until the rice is hot and sticky. Serve with 2 tablespoons toasted coconut shavings or shredded dried coconut and steamed broccoli.

2 **Curried Sweet Potato and Coconut Soup** Heat 3 tablespoons vegetable oil in a large, nonstick saucepan or casserole. Add 3 medium sweet potatoes (about 1¼ lb), peeled and cubed, a 1-inch piece of fresh ginger root, peeled and finely chopped, 2 thinly sliced garlic cloves, 1 teaspoon cumin seeds, and 1 seeded and chopped red chile, if using, and sauté gently for 5–6 minutes, until lightly golden. Add 2 tablespoons Thai red curry paste and 1¾ cups coconut milk and cook for 2 minutes. Add 4 cups hot vegetable stock, then bring to a boil and simmer gently for about 12 minutes, until the potatoes are tender. Use a handheld immersion blender to blend the soup until smooth, then ladle into deep bowls. Serve sprinkled with 2 tablespoons toasted coconut shavings or shredded dried coconut.

Bulgur Wheat with Goat Cheese and Red Onion

Serves 4

3¼ cups hot
  vegetable stock
2 cups bulgur wheat
¼ cup olive oil or vegetable oil
1 large red onion, halved and
  thinly sliced
½ cup tomato juice
2 tablespoons lime juice
1 cup crumbled firm goat cheese
3 tablespoons coarsely chopped
  flat leaf parsley
salt and pepper

- Bring the vegetable stock to a boil in a large saucepan, add the bulgur wheat, and cook for 7 minutes. Remove from the heat, cover with a tight-fitting lid, and set aside for 5–8 minutes, until the liquid has been absorbed and the grains are tender.

- Meanwhile, heat 2 tablespoons of oil in a skillet and cook the onion gently for 7–8 minutes, until soft and golden.

- Combine the remaining oil with the tomato juice and lime juice, and season with salt and pepper. Fold the dressing, onion, goat cheese, and parsley into the bulgur wheat with a fork, and spoon the mixture into 4 shallow bowls to serve.

Goat Cheese Couscous Place 1¼ cups couscous in a bowl with 1 tablespoon of olive oil or vegetable oil and a generous pinch of salt. Pour 1¼ cups boiling vegetable stock over the couscous and set aside for 5–8 minutes, until the grains are tender and the liquid has been absorbed. Meanwhile, combine 3 tablespoons oil with ½ cup tomato juice and 2 tablespoons lime juice and season with salt and pepper. Fold the goat cheese and parsley into the couscous, then spoon the mixture into serving bowls. Drizzle with the dressing and sprinkle with 3 sliced scallions to serve.

Goat Cheese Pockets with Bulgur Wheat Salad Roll out 1 sheet store-bought puff pastry and cut into quarters. Crumble 6 oz firm goat cheese and place some cheese in the center of each quarter, then divide 8 halved cherry tomatoes and 2 thinly sliced scallions among them. Fold the sides of the pastry quarters in toward the center, so that the filling is not quite covered, and pinch together the sides to seal. Cook in a preheated oven, at 350°F, for 18–20 minutes, until crisp and golden. Meanwhile, prepare the bulgur wheat following the main recipe but omitting the goat cheese. Spoon the bulgur onto 4 serving plates and serve with the goat cheese pockets.

Chickpea and Spinach Omelet

Serves 4

2 tablespoons olive oil

1 large onion, sliced

1 red bell pepper, sliced

½ teaspoon hot smoked paprika or sweet paprika

1 (15 oz) can chickpeas, drained and rinsed

3½ cups fresh spinach, rinsed, trimmed, and coarsely sliced

5 eggs, lightly beaten

¾ cup coarsely chopped, pitted green olives

1⅓ cups shredded cheddar cheese

salt and pepper

- Heat the olive oil in a large, nonstick skillet. Add the onion and bell pepper and cook gently for 7–8 minutes, until soft and golden. Stir in the paprika and chickpeas and cook for 1 minute, stirring frequently. Add the spinach and cook until just wilted.

- Pour the beaten eggs into the skillet and stir to combine. Cook gently, without stirring, for 4–5 minutes, until almost set.

- Sprinkle with the olives and grated cheddar, then slide under a preheated hot broiler, keeping the handle away from the heat. Broil for 4–5 minutes, until golden and set. Slice into wedges and serve immediately.

Chickpea and Spinach Salad with Poached Eggs Heat 2 tablespoons olive oil in a large skillet. Add 1 sliced onion and 1 sliced red bell pepper and cook gently for 7–8 minutes. Stir in ½ teaspoon hot smoked paprika or sweet paprika and 1 (15 oz) can chickpeas, drained and rinsed, and cook for 1 minute, stirring frequently. Meanwhile, poach 4 eggs in a large saucepan of gently simmering water. Toss the chickpea mixture briefly with 1 (6 oz) package baby spinach and mound onto 4 serving plates. Top each salad with a poached egg and serve immediately.

Chickpea Casserole with Garlic Bread Heat 2 tablespoons olive oil in a large, nonstick skillet. Cook 1 large sliced onion and 1 sliced red bell pepper gently for 4–5 minutes, then add 2 chopped garlic cloves and cook for an additional 3 minutes, until soft and golden. Stir in 1 (14½ oz) can diced tomatoes, ⅔ cup hot water or vegetable stock, 1 (15 oz) can chickpeas, drained and rinsed, and ¾ cup coarsely chopped, pitted green olives and simmer gently for 12–15 minutes, until thick and rich. Meanwhile, wash, trim, and coarsely slice 8 oz fresh spinach and cook 8 store-bought garlic bread slices according to the package directions. Stir the spinach into the chickpeas and cook for 1–2 minutes, until just wilted, then season with salt and pepper. Spoon into 4 bowls and serve with the hot, crusty garlic bread.

30 Chili con Verduda

Serves 4

2 tablespoons vegetable oil
1 carrot, finely chopped
1 celery stick, finely chopped
1 onion, chopped
2 garlic cloves, chopped
1 teaspoon ground cumin
1 teaspoon ground coriander
½ teaspoon ground cinnamon
½ teaspoon dried red pepper flakes
1 (15 oz) can kidney beans
⅔ cup frozen peas
1 (14½ oz) can tomatoes
2 tablespoons tomato paste
1 cup lager-style beer or
   vegetable stock
salt and pepper
2 tablespoons chopped cilantro,
   to garnish
soft flour tortillas and shredded
   cheddar cheese, to serve

- Heat the oil in a large saucepan or casserole and add the carrots, celery, onion, and garlic. Cook for 8 minutes, until beginning to soften.

- Stir in the ground spices and red pepper flakes and cook for an additional minute, stirring continuously. Drain and rinse the kidney beans, then put in the pan along with all the remaining ingredients and bring to a boil. Reduce the heat, cover, and simmer gently for 15–20 minutes, until thickened and tender. Season to taste, scatter with chopped cilantro, and serve with warm soft tortillas and grated cheddar.

---

10 Chili Bean Tortillas

Heat 2 tablespoons olive oil or vegetable oil in a large skillet and cook 1 finely chopped onion, 1 chopped red bell pepper, and 2 chopped garlic cloves for 4–5 minutes, until lightly browned. Add 1 teaspoon ground cumin, 1 teaspoon ground coriander, and ½ teaspoon each ground cinnamon and dried red pepper flakes, and cook for 1 minute, then pour in 1 (10 oz) jar spicy tomato salsa and 1 (15 oz) can kidney beans, drained and rinsed. Simmer gently for 2–3 minutes. Meanwhile, heat 1 tablespoon oil in a large skillet and cook 4 extra-large eggs for 2–3 minutes, until the white is set and the yolk still runny. Toast 4 large soft flour tortillas and place 1 on each of 4 serving plates. Spoon over the spicy beans and top each one with a fried egg. Serve immediately.

20 Quick Veggie Chili

Cook the onion, red bell pepper, and garlic following the 10-minute recipe. Stir in 1 (1¼ oz) envelope chili con carne seasoning mix, ⅔ cup frozen peas, 1 (15 oz) can kidney beans, drained and rinsed, 1 (14½ oz) can tomatoes, 2 tablespoons tomato paste, and ½ cup lager or vegetable stock. Simmer for 10–15 minutes. Serve with 4 warm flour tortillas, shredded cheddar cheese, and chopped cilantro.

Basil and Arugula Pesto with Whole-Wheat Spaghetti

Serves 4

¼ cup sunflower seeds or pumpkin seeds
16 oz whole-wheat spaghetti
1 small garlic clove, coarsely chopped
1 small bunch of basil
3 cups arugula
¼ cup grated Parmesan-style cheese, plus extra to serve (optional)
⅓ cup olive oil
1 tablespoon lemon juice
coarse sea salt and pepper

- Place the seeds in a small, dry skillet and toast gently for 3–4 minutes, shaking the skillet frequently, until lightly toasted and golden. Transfer to a plate to cool.

- Cook the spaghetti in a large saucepan of lightly salted boiling water according to the package directions, until al dente.

- Meanwhile, crush the garlic together with a generous pinch of sea salt, using a mortar and pestle. Add the basil and arugula and pound until crushed to a coarse paste.

- Add the toasted seeds and pound to a paste, then transfer to a bowl and stir in the cheese, olive oil, and lemon juice. Season with plenty of black pepper and more salt, if necessary.

- Drain the pasta and toss immediately with the pesto. Divide among 4 shallow bowls and serve with extra cheese, if desired.

 Quick Basil and Arugula Pesto

Cook 16 oz quick-cook pasta according to the package directions. Place ¼ cup toasted sunflower seeds or pumpkin seeds in a mini chopper or the small bowl of a food processor with 1 coarsely chopped clove of garlic, 1 bunch of basil, and 3 cups arugula. Season, pulse until finely chopped, then transfer to a bowl and stir in ¼ cup grated Parmesan-style cheese, ⅓ cup olive oil, and 1 tablespoon lemon juice. Drain the pasta well, toss with the pesto, and serve immediately.

 Creamy Gnocchi Pesto Casserole

Cook 16 oz store-bought fresh gnocchi in a large saucepan of lightly salted boiling water for about 2 minutes, or according to the package directions, until just tender. Meanwhile, make the pesto following the 10-minute recipe, then stir in 1¼ cups crème fraîche. Stir in the cooked gnocchi, then transfer to a large ovenproof dish and sprinkle with 2 tablespoons grated Parmesan-style cheese. Cook in a preheated oven, at 375°F, for about 20 minutes, until bubbling and golden. Serve with extra arugula, if desired.

30 Mustardy Squash, Carrot, and Sweet Potato Casserole

Serves 4

3 tablespoons vegetable oil
1 red onion, coarsely chopped
4 garlic cloves, chopped
1½ lb butternut squash,
    peeled, seeded, and cut
    into bite-size chunks
3 medium sweet potatoes
    (about 1 lb), peeled and cut
    into bite-size chunks
2 carrots, peeled and cut into
    bite-size chunks
½ cup dry white wine
1 teaspoon dried tarragon
    or rosemary
1¾ cup hot vegetable stock
2 tablespoons whole-grain mustard
4 cups rinsed, trimmed, and
    chopped fresh spinach
salt and pepper
steamed rice, to serve

- Heat the oil in a heavy saucepan or casserole. Cook the onion and garlic for 3–4 minutes, until softened. Add the squash, sweet potato, and carrot, and cook for an additional 3–4 minutes, until lightly golden.

- Pour in the wine and herbs and reduce by half. Add the vegetable stock and mustard to the pan, then season generously, bring to a boil, and simmer gently for about 15 minutes, until the vegetables are tender.

- Stir in the spinach and cook until wilted, then serve in bowls with steamed couscous or rice.

 Mustardy Carrot Salad Peel and shred 4 carrots and place in a large bowl with ½ red onion, finely chopped, and 3½ cups baby spinach leaves. Combine 3 tablespoons olive oil or vegetable oil in a small bowl with 1 tablespoon mustard, 1 small crushed garlic clove, 1 teaspoon freshly chopped tarragon or rosemary, and 2 teaspoons white wine vinegar. Whisk to combine and season to taste. Toss with the carrot salad and serve immediately.

Mustardy Mashed Squash and Sweet Potatoes Cook 1½ lb butternut squash, peeled, seeded, and cut into bite-size chunks, 3 medium sweet potatoes (about 1 lb), peeled and cubed, and 4 whole garlic cloves in a large saucepan of lightly salted boiling water or vegetable stock for about 15 minutes, until just tender. Drain and return to the pan with 4 tablespoons butter, 2 tablespoons whole-grain mustard, and 2 tablespoons freshly chopped parsley, if desired. Mash until almost smooth, then season with salt and pepper. Serve the mustardy mashed vegetables with wilted spinach leaves and cooked veggie sausages.

Aloo Tikki with Cilantro and Mint Chutney

Serves 4

6 medium potatoes (about 1½ lb), peeled and cut into chunks
¼ cup chopped fresh cilantro
2 teaspoons finely grated fresh ginger root
2½ teaspoons garam masala
1 green chile, chopped and seeded
½ cup frozen peas, defrosted
⅓ (10 oz) package frozen spinach, defrosted
2 tablespoons chopped mint
1 cup plain yogurt
2 teaspoons lemon juice
1⅔ cups fresh bread crumbs
2–3 tablespoons all-purpose flour
vegetable oil, for pan-frying
salt and pepper

- Cook the potatoes in a large saucepan of lightly salted boiling water for about 10 minutes or until just tender. Drain well.

- Meanwhile, mix half the cilantro with the grated ginger, garam masala, chopped chile, and peas. Place the spinach in the middle of a clean dish towel, bring up the edges, and twist the spinach in the towel over a sink to squeeze out the excess moisture. Add to the bowl of spices, season generously with salt and pepper, and mix well to combine. Set aside.

- To make the chutney, mix the remaining cilantro with the mint, yogurt, and lemon juice, season, and set aside.

- Add the potatoes to the spinach and peas and mash well to combine. Add the bread crumbs and mix thoroughly to form a soft dough mixture. Form into 20–24 small patties and dust in the flour.

- Heat the oil in a large skillet and pan-fry the patties for 3–4 minutes, turning once, until crisp and golden. Drain on paper towels and serve with the chutney.

---

1 **Stuffed Naan with Cilantro and Mint Chutney** Heat 2 tablespoons oil in a large, nonstick skillet and cook 2 teaspoons finely grated fresh ginger root, 1 chopped and seeded green chile, and 2 crushed garlic cloves gently for 1–2 minutes, until lightly golden. Wash, trim, and coarsely chop 8 oz fresh spinach and add to the skillet with 1⅓ cups frozen peas, 2½ teaspoons garam masala, 2 tablespoons lemon juice, and 2 tablespoons chopped fresh cilantro. Season generously and cook for 3–4 minutes, until the peas are just tender and the spinach wilted. Make the chutney following the main recipe. Split open 4 large naans and spoon the spiced pea and spinach mixture into them. Serve with the cilantro and mint chutney.

 2 **Potato and Spinach Curry with Cilantro** Cook the ginger, chile, and garlic following the 10-minute recipe. Add 6 medium potatoes (about 1½ lb), peeled and cut into cubes, 2½ teaspoons garam masala, and 2 tablespoons medium curry paste and cook for 2 minutes. Add 4 diced tomatoes and 1½ cups hot vegetable stock, cover, and simmer for 12 minutes. Add 8 oz rinsed and trimmed spinach and cook for 1–2 minutes. Serve topped with plain yogurt and chopped cilantro.

10 Feta, Scallion, and Walnut Mini Tarts

Serves 4

4 slices wheat bread,
  crusts removed
1 cup crumbled feta cheese
2 scallions, thinly sliced
¼ cup walnut pieces,
  lightly crushed
8 cherry tomatoes,
  cut into quarters
1 tablespoon olive oil
salt and pepper

To serve

1 (7 oz) package mixed
  salad greens
½ cucumber, sliced

- Preheat the oven to 400°F. Use a rolling pin to roll the bread out thinly. Cut each slice into a circle, approximately 5 inches in diameter, and press the circles into 4 large, nonstick muffin pans. Cook in the preheated oven for 7–8 minutes, until crisp and golden.

- Meanwhile, mix the crumbled feta with the scallions, walnut pieces, and tomatoes. Season to taste, then spoon the mixture into the toasted tart shells. Drizzle with the olive oil and serve with a mixed salad greens and cucumber salad.

20 Feta, Scallion, and Walnut Pasta Salad

Cook 1 lb whole-wheat penne in a large saucepan of lightly salted boiling water according to the package directions, until al dente. Meanwhile, place 1⅓ cups crumbled feta cheese in a large bowl with 4 thinly sliced scallions, ½ cup walnut pieces, and 12 quartered cherry tomatoes. Drain the pasta and refresh under cold running water. Drain well and transfer to the bowl with 2 tablespoons lemon juice, 2 tablespoons olive oil, and plenty of black pepper. Toss to combine and mound into bowls to serve.

30 Feta, Scallion, and Walnut Tart

Roll out 1 sheet store-bought puff pastry. Place on a lightly greased baking sheet and score a border about ¾ inch in from the edges all the way around the pastry, not quite cutting through. Sprinkle 1¹⁄₃ cups crumbled feta cheese, 4 thinly sliced scallions, ½ cup walnut pieces, and 12 quartered cherry tomatoes over the pastry, keeping within the border. Drizzle with 1 tablespoon olive oil and cook in a preheated oven, at 400°F, for about 20 minutes, until crisp and golden. Serve with a salad, if desired.

Tomato and Mascarpone Penne Pasta

Serves 4

2 cups tomato puree
1 garlic clove, crushed
2 tablespoons olive oil
½ teaspoon sugar
1 teaspoon dried oregano
1 teaspoon finely grated lemon
  rind (optional)
1 lb penne pasta
⅔ cup mascarpone or
  cream cheese
salt and pepper

- Pour the tomato puree into a saucepan with the garlic, olive oil, sugar, oregano, and lemon rind, if using. Cover loosely with a lid, bring to a boil, then simmer gently for 15 minutes.

- Meanwhile, cook the pasta in a large saucepan of lightly salted boiling water for 11 minutes, or according to the package directions, until al dente. Drain and return to the pan.

- Stir the mascarpone into the pasta sauce, season lightly with salt and pepper, then pour over the pasta. Stir briefly to combine and serve immediately in shallow bowls.

Quick Tomato and Mascarpone Pasta

Sauce Cook 1 lb quick-cook pasta shapes in a saucepan of lightly salted boiling water for 3–5 minutes, or according to the package directions, until al dente. Meanwhile, heat 1 (14–15 oz) jar tomato-based pasta sauce until warmed through. Stir ⅔ cup mascarpone or cream cheese into the sauce, with 1 small bunch of chopped basil, if desired. Serve hot with the drained pasta.

Tomato and Mascarpone

Casserole Cook 1 lb quick-cook pasta shapes in a saucepan of lightly salted boiling water for 3 minutes, or according to the package directions, until almost al dente. Meanwhile, combine 2 cups tomato puree, 1 crushed garlic clove, 2 tablespoons olive oil, ½ teaspoon sugar, 1 teaspoon dried oregano, and 1 teaspoon finely grated lemon rind, if using, in a large saucepan and place over medium heat until simmering gently. Drain the pasta and stir into the sauce. Transfer to a large ovenproof dish and sprinkle with 1⅓ cups shredded cheddar cheese. Cook in a preheated oven, at 400°F, for 20–25 minutes, until bubbling and golden. Spoon into dishes and serve with extra cheese, if desired.

Brie and Thyme Melts

Serves 4

1 ciabatta-style loaf, cut in half horizontally

⅓ cup onion chutney or carmelized onion chutney (or 1 onion, sliced and sautéed)

8 oz Brie or Camembert cheese, sliced

1 teaspoon dried thyme

4 teaspoons chili oil, garlic oil, or basil oil

tomato salad, to serve (optional)

- Cut the two pieces of bread in half to make 4 servings. Arrange, cut side up, on a baking sheet and spread each piece with the onion chutney.

- Lay the Brie slices on top and sprinkle with the thyme. Drizzle with the flavored oil and cook under a preheated broiler for 3–4 minutes, until the cheese begins to melt. Serve immediately with a tomato salad, if desired.

 Whole Baked Cheese with Garlic and Thyme Cut some little slits in the top of a whole 8 oz round Camembert or Brie. Insert 1 thinly sliced garlic clove and 5–6 little thyme sprigs into the slits. Drizzle with 2 teaspoons chili oil, garlic oil, or basil oil, then wrap in a loose foil package and cook in a preheated oven, at 350°F, for about 15 minutes, until soft and oozing. Serve with toasted ciabatta, onion chutney, if desired, and a tomato salad.

 Brie, Thyme, and Onion Pizza Place 1 sheet rolled piecrust dough on a large greased baking sheet and fold in the edges by about ½ inch to create a crust. Spread with ⅓ cup onion chutney or sautéed onions, then top with 8 oz sliced Brie or Camembert cheese. Sprinkle with 1 teaspoon dried thyme and drizzle with 4 teaspoons chili oil, garlic oil, or basil oil. Cook in a preheated oven, at 400°F, for about 20 minutes, until the pastry is crisp and golden and the cheese has melted. Serve with a tomato salad.

30 Bean Burgers with Garlicky Yogurt

Serves 4

3 tablespoons vegetable oil
1 onion, finely chopped
1 garlic clove, chopped
1 (15 oz) can kidney beans,
   drained and rinsed
1 (15 oz) can black-eyed peas,
   drained and rinsed
1 tablespoon tomato paste
1 teaspoon paprika (optional)
¼ cup finely chopped
   flat leaf parsley
1 medium egg, lightly beaten
2 cup fresh white bread crumbs
1 cup plain yogurt
1 small garlic clove, crushed
2 teaspoons lemon juice
salt and pepper
4 soft flour tortillas, warmed,
   to serve
lettuce leaves, to garnish

- Heat 2 tablespoons of the oil in a small skillet and cook the onion gently for 6–7 minutes. Add the chopped garlic and cook for an additional 2–3 minutes, until really soft and golden.

- Meanwhile, place both types of beans in the large bowl of a food processor with the tomato paste, paprika, if using, and half the parsley. Pulse until the mixture becomes a coarse paste. Transfer to a bowl and add the egg, bread crumbs, and cooked onion mixture. Season with salt and pepper, then mix well and shape into 4 large patties.

- Heat the remaining oil in a large nonstick skillet and cook the burgers gently for 8–10 minutes, turning once, until crisp and golden.

- Meanwhile, mix the yogurt with the crushed garlic, the remaining parsley, and the lemon juice. Season with salt and pepper and set aside.

- Serve the burgers with warm tortillas and the yogurt and garnish with lettuce leaves.

 Mixed Bean Hummus Put 2 cups drained and rinsed canned mixed beans, such as chickpeas, kidney beans, and pinto beans, into a food processor. Add 1 tablespoon tomato paste, 1 teaspoon paprika, ¼ cup chopped flat leaf parsley, 1 small crushed garlic clove, and 2 teaspoons lemon juice and blend to a paste. Add enough yogurt to form a smooth, creamy consistency, season, and serve with raw vegetables for dipping.

Mixed Bean Tortilla Pockets Make Mixed Bean Hummus, following the 10-minute recipe. Divide the hummus among 4 large, soft flour tortillas and top with 1 sliced red bell pepper, 1 thinly sliced celery stick, ½ a thinly sliced red onion, and 1 cup shredded cheddar cheese. Fold the sides of the tortillas over to form 4 neat packages and toast on a preheated hot griddle pan for about 8 minutes, turning once, until hot and lightly charred. Serve immediately with shredded iceberg lettuce and salsa, if desired.

BUD-VEGG-SED

30 Baked Bell Peppers with Feta and Scallions

Serves 4

4 red or yellow bell peppers
4 small tomatoes, halved
8 oz feta cheese, sliced
3 scallions, finely sliced
2 tablespoons olive oil or
   vegetable oil, plus extra
   for greasing
1¼ cups couscous
2 tablespoons butter
1¼ cups boiling vegetable stock
   or water
freshly ground black pepper
2 tablespoons pumpkin seeds or
   sunflower seeds, to garnish
   (optional)

- Preheat the oven to 400°F and lightly grease a baking sheet. Cut the bell peppers in half lengthwise and remove the seeds and cores. Place all 8 halves on the baking sheet and fill with the tomato halves and the slices of feta and scallions. Season with black pepper, drizzle with the oil, and cook in the preheated oven for 20–25 minutes, until softened and golden.

- Meanwhile, put the couscous into a bowl with the butter and pour over a boiling stock. Cover and set aside for 5–8 minutes, until the liquid has been absorbed and the grains are tender.

- Serve the baked bell peppers with the couscous, sprinkled with pumpkin or sunflower seeds, if using.

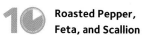 **Roasted Pepper, Feta, and Scallion Salad** Follow the main recipe to prepare 1¼ cups couscous. Meanwhile, drain 1 (12 oz) jar roasted red peppers and remove any seeds. Slice the flesh into strips and toss gently with 8 oz sliced feta cheese and 3 finely sliced scallions. Cut 4 small tomatoes into wedges. Spoon the couscous onto 4 plates and top with the tomato and roasted red pepper mixture. Sprinkle with 2 tablespoons pumpkin seeds or sunflower seeds to serve.

 Roasted Pepper, Feta, and Scallion Tabbouleh Put 1¼ cups couscous into a bowl with 2 tablespoons butter and pour 1¼ cups boiling vegetable stock or water over the grains. Cover and set aside for 5–8 minutes, until the liquid has been absorbed and the grains are tender. Use a fork to fluff up the grains, then spread the couscous over a large baking sheet to cool. Meanwhile, finely dice 1 red bell pepper and 1 yellow bell pepper, then seed and finely dice 2 ripe but firm tomatoes. Thinly slice 4 scallions and finely chop 1 large bunch of flat leaf parsley. Fold all the ingredients into the cooled couscous with 2 tablespoons each of lemon juice and olive oil. Spoon into shallow dishes and crumble 8 oz feta cheese over the top. Serve sprinkled with the 2 tablespoons pumpkin seeds or sunflower seeds, if using.

BUD-VEGG-PIU

30 Marinated Tofu with Vegetables

Serves 4

3 tablespoons ketjap manis
   or sweet soy sauce
1 teaspoon crushed garlic
2 teaspoons minced ginger
2 tablespoons sweet chili
   dipping sauce
16 oz firm tofu, cut into
   ¾-inch slices
2 tablespoons vegetable oil
   or peanut oil
1 carrot, peeled and cut into
   fine matchsticks
1 lb bok choy, sliced
2 cups bean sprouts
1 (8 oz) can bamboo
   shoots in water
⅓ cup oyster sauce
2 teaspoons sesame seeds,
   to garnish (optional)

- Mix the ketjap manis, garlic, ginger, and sweet chili dipping sauce in a small bowl. Arrange the tofu slices in a shallow dish and pour the marinade over the slices, turning to coat. Set aside to marinate for about 20 minutes.

- Carefully transfer the tofu slices to a foil-lined broiler rack, reserving the marinade. Cook under a preheated broiler for about 3 minutes on each side, until golden. Remove from the heat and keep warm.

- Meanwhile, heat the oil in a wok over moderate heat. Stir-fry the carrot and bok choy for 4–5 minutes, until beginning to soften. Add the bean sprouts and bamboo shoots and cook for 1 minute, then pour in the remaining marinade and the oyster sauce.

- Spoon the vegetables into deep bowls, top with the broiled tofu slices, and sprinkle with golden sesame seeds, if using.

 **Marinated Tofu Stir-Fry**

Heat 2 tablespoons vegetable oil or peanut oil in a wok and stir-fry 1 (16 oz) package mixed stir-fry vegetables for 4–5 minutes, until beginning to soften. Pour in 1 cup store-bought Chinese oyster and scallion sauce and cook until hot. Divide among 4 deep bowls, then top with 1 cup prepared marinated tofu strips. Serve sprinkled with sesame seeds, if using.

 Tofu and Vegetable Noodles

Cook the stir-fried vegetables following the main recipe, adding 1 cup prepared tofu strips or cubed firm tofu, along with the bean sprouts and bamboo shoots. Meanwhile, cook 8 oz medium dried egg noodles according to the package directions, then drain and toss with the vegetables and tofu. Serve with soy sauce.

3 Roasted Butternut Couscous with Cheese

Serves 4

2 lb butternut squash, peeled and cut into bite-size pieces

3 tablespoons olive oil or vegetable oil

1 teaspoon dried red pepper flakes

1 teaspoon fennel seeds

1¼ cups couscous

1¼ cups boiling vegetable stock or water

8 oz Wensleydale, cheddar, or a white crumbly cheese

2 scallions, finely sliced

2 tablespoons toasted pine nuts (optional)

salt and pepper

· Preheat the oven to 425°F. Parboil the squash in a large saucepan of lightly salted water for 5–7 minutes. Drain really well and transfer to a roasting pan. Drizzle with 2 tablespoons of the oil, sprinkle with the red pepper flakes and fennel seeds, then season generously with salt and pepper. Cook in the preheated oven for 18–20 minutes, until tender.

· Meanwhile, place the couscous in a large bowl. Stir in the remaining oil and a generous pinch of salt. Add the boiling stock, then cover and set aside for 5–10 minutes, until the grains are tender and all the liquid has been absorbed.

· Spoon the couscous onto 4 plates, top with the roasted butternut squash, and crumble the cheese over the top. Sprinkle with the scallions and pine nuts, if using, and serve immediately.

 Roasted-Style Couscous with Cheese Heat 3 tablespoons oil in a skillet and cook 1¼ cups couscous for 1–2 minutes, stirring continuously. Add 2 sliced scallions and 1 teaspoon dried red pepper flakes. Season and cook for an additional minute. Pour in 1¼ cups hot vegetable stock, remove from the heat, and cover tightly for 5–6 minutes, until the grains are tender and the liquid has been absorbed. Spoon into bowls, top with 2 cups shredded cheddar, and sprinkle with 2 tablespoons toasted pine nuts, if desired.

 Root Vegetable Couscous with Parmesan Cheese Cook 4 each of carrots and parsnips, peeled and cut into chunks, in a large saucepan of lightly salted boiling water for 10–12 minutes, until tender. Heat 2 tablespoons olive oil in a large, nonstick skillet, and cook the carrots and parsnips with 1 teaspoon dried red pepper flakes and 1 teaspoon fennel seeds over high heat for 5–6 minutes, until lightly golden. Season to taste. Meanwhile, follow the main recipe to cook 1¼ cups couscous. Spoon the vegetables over the couscous, and serve topped with ½ cups grated Parmesan-style cheese.

 # Spicy Kidney Beans with Rice

Serves 4

1⅓ cups long-grain rice

2 tablespoons olive oil or
  vegetable oil

1 large red onion, chopped

1 red bell pepper, cored, seeded,
  and chopped

2 celery sticks, chopped

2 teaspoons Cajun- or Mexican-
  style spice blend

2 (15 oz) cans red kidney beans,
  drained and rinsed

3 ripe tomatoes, diced

1 tablespoon red wine vinegar

1 teaspoon Tabasco sauce, plus
  extra to serve

½ cup water

salt and pepper

2 tablespoons chopped chives,
  to garnish (optional)

¼ cup crème fraîche,
  to serve (optional)

- Bring a large saucepan of lightly salted water to a boil and cook the rice according to the package directions, until just tender. Drain and keep hot.

- Meanwhile, heat the oil in a large, deep skillet and add the onion, bell pepper, and celery. Cook for 8–9 minutes, until softened. Add the spice mix, cook for 1 minute, then stir in the kidney beans, tomatoes, vinegar, Tabasco, and measured water.

- Cover and simmer gently for 7–8 minutes, adding a little more water, if necessary. Season and sprinkle with the chopped chives, if using. Serve with the tender rice, extra Tabasco, and crème fraîche, if desired.

---

1 Spicy Mexican Rice Salad Finely chop 1 red bell pepper and mix with ½ finely chopped red onion and 2 finely chopped celery sticks. Stir in 2 cups cooked wild and long-grain rice and 1 (15 oz) can kidney beans, rinsed and drained. Add 2 seeded and chopped tomatoes, 2 tablespoons chopped chives, and 2 tablespoons lime juice. Season generously and serve with tortilla chips.

3 One-Dish Spicy Mexican Rice Heat 2 tablespoons olive oil or vegetable oil in a large saucepan or casserole and cook 1 chopped red onion, 1 chopped red bell pepper, and 2 chopped celery sticks over medium-high heat for about 5 minutes, until slightly browned. Stir in 1⅓ cups rinsed long-grain rice and 2 teaspoons Mexican-style spice mix and cook for 1 minute, then add 1 tablespoon tomato paste, 1 (14½ oz) can diced tomatoes, 1 (15 oz) can kidney beans, drained and rinsed, and 2½ cups boiling vegetable stock. Reduce the heat, cover with a tight-fitting lid, and simmer gently for 20–23 minutes, until the rice is tender and the liquid has been absorbed. Serve with Tabasco and sour cream, and sprinkle with chopped chives, if desired.

30 Potato and Onion Pizza

Serves 4

2⅓ cups all-purpose flour

2¼ teaspoons (1 envelope)
active dry yeast

1½ teaspoons sugar

1 teaspoon salt

¾ cup warm water

3 tablespoons olive oil, plus extra
for greasing

½ cup crème fraîche

6 unpeeled new potatoes,
thinly sliced on a mandolin

½ onion, thinly sliced
on a mandolin

2 teaspoons dried thyme

1⅓ cups shredded Swiss cheese
or cheddar cheese

12 ripe black olives (optional)

cracked black pepper

- Preheat the oven to 400°F and lightly grease a baking sheet. In a large bowl, mix together the flour, yeast, sugar, and salt. Make a well in the center and pour in the warm water and 2 tablespoons of the oil. Combine to make a soft dough, then roll out to a rectangle about 14 x 10 inches. Transfer to the baking sheet and cook in the preheated oven for 5 minutes or until just beginning to brown.

- Spoon ¼ cup of the crème fraîche over the pizza crust. Top with the slices of potato and onion, then sprinkle with the thyme and cheese. Drizzle the remaining oil over the pizza and return to the oven. Increase the temperature to 425°F and bake for about 15 minutes, until golden.

- Cut the pizza into slices, sprinkle with the olives, if desired, and top with the remaining crème fraîche. Season with cracked black pepper and serve hot.

 Creamy Potato and Onion Gnocchi

Heat 2 tablespoons olive oil in a skillet and cook 1 chopped onion and 2 chopped garlic cloves for 7–8 minutes. Meanwhile, cook 1 (16 oz) package gnocchi according to the package directions. Add 1¾ cups crème fraîche, 1 teaspoon thyme leaves, and 1⅓ cups shredded Swiss cheese or cheddar cheese to the onion and stir for 1 minute. Season generously and stir in the drained gnocchi. Spoon into 4 bowls and serve immediately, with extra cheese, if desired.

 Potato and Onion Gratin Cook 2 lb thinly sliced potatoes in a large saucepan of lightly salted boiling water for 8–10 minutes, until just tender. Drain well and transfer to a large, heat-resistant bowl. Meanwhile, heat 2 tablespoons of olive oil in a skillet, and sauté 1 thinly sliced onion and 2 chopped garlic cloves for 6–7 minutes, until lightly golden. Stir in 2 cups crème fraîche, 1 teaspoon dried thyme, and plenty of salt and pepper. Bring to a boil, then remove from the heat. Pour the sauce over the potatoes, shaking gently to combine, then transfer to a large ovenproof dish. Sprinkle with 1⅓ cups shredded Swiss cheese or cheddar cheese and cook under a preheated moderate broiler for 6–8 minutes, until bubbling and golden. Serve with a green salad, sprinkled with 12 ripe black olives, if desired.

30 Lentil Bolognese

Serves 4

1 onion, coarsely chopped
1 carrot, peeled and chopped
1 celery stick, coarsely chopped
1 garlic clove, peeled
3 tablespoons olive oil
½ cup red wine
½ cup water
¼ cup tomato paste
1 (14½ oz) can diced tomatoes
1 teaspoon dried mixed herbs
2 (15½ oz) cans lentils, drained
    and rinsed, or 4 cups
    cooked lentils
salt and pepper

To serve

½ cup grated Parmesan-style
    cheese
crusty bread

- Place the onion, carrot, celery, and garlic in a food processor and pulse briefly until finely chopped. Heat the olive oil in a large, heavy casserole or saucepan. Add the vegetable mixture and cook for 5–6 minutes, stirring frequently, until softened and lightly golden.

- Pour in the red wine, measured water, tomato paste, diced tomatoes, and herbs, and season with salt and pepper. Simmer gently for about 15 minutes, then add the lentils and simmer for an additional 5–7 minutes, until thickened and tender. Spoon into deep bowls, sprinkle with cheese, and serve with plenty of fresh, crusty bread.

---

10 Quick Lentil Bolognese

Place 1 coarsely chopped onion, 1 peeled and coarsely chopped carrot, 1 coarsely chopped celery stick, and 1 garlic clove in a food processor and pulse until finely chopped. Heat 3 tablespoons olive oil in a large, heavy casserole or saucepan and cook the vegetable mixture for 5–6 minutes, stirring frequently, until softened and lightly golden. Stir in 2 cups store-bought tomato pasta sauce and 2 (15½ oz) cans lentils, drained and rinsed, or 4 cups cooked lentils. Simmer gently for 2–3 minutes, then serve as above, with Parmesan-style cheese and crusty bread.

20 Green Lentil and Vegetable Soup

Cook the vegetables following the 10-minute recipe, then add 1 (14½ oz) can diced tomatoes, 1 teaspoon dried mixed herbs, 2 (15½ oz) cans lentils, drained and rinsed, or 4 cups cooked lentils, and 4 cups hot vegetable stock. Season well, bring to a boil, and simmer for 12–15 minutes, until tender. Use a handheld immersion blender to blend until smooth, then ladle the soup into bowls and serve with ½ cup grated Parmesan-style cheese.

20 Homemade Baked Beans

Serves 4

2 tablespoons olive oil or
  vegetable oil
1 onion, thinly sliced
2 garlic cloves, crushed
2 cups tomato puree
½ cup hot vegetable stock
  or water
½ teaspoon sugar
2 (15 oz) cans navy beans, drained
  and rinsed
pinch of cayenne (optional)
pinch of cinnamon (optional)
salt and pepper
4 thick slices of whole-grain
  bread, to serve

- Heat the olive oil in a heavy saucepan and cook the onion gently for 3–4 minutes. Add the garlic and cook for an additional 2 minutes, until softened and golden.

- Add the tomato puree, stock, sugar, beans, and spices, if using, and season with salt and pepper. Simmer gently for 12–14 minutes, until rich and thick.

- Meanwhile, toast the bread until golden and place on 4 plates. Serve the beans spooned over the toast.

---

10 Crunchy Bean Salad

Place 2 (15 oz) cans navy beans, drained and rinsed, in a bowl and add 3 diced tomatoes, 1 crushed garlic clove, 1 finely chopped red onion, 3 tablespoons oil, a pinch of sugar, and 1 tablespoon red wine vinegar. Stir to combine, then spoon into bowls and serve topped with 3 cups store-bought croutons.

30 Crispy-Topped Baked Beans

Make the baked beans following the main recipe, adding an extra ¼ cup vegetable stock or water. Meanwhile, melt 2 tablespoons butter in a skillet with 3 cups fresh bread crumbs. Stir over low heat for 5–6 minutes, until beginning to crisp, then transfer to a bowl with 2 tablespoons chopped fresh parsley and 2 tablespoons grated Parmesan-style cheese. Transfer the beans to a large ovenproof dish and sprinkle the bread crumb topping over the top. Cook in a preheated oven, at 400°F, for about 10 minutes, until the topping is crisp and lightly golden. Serve with green salad.

30 Chunky Vegetable and Cheese Gratin

Serves 4

1 stick butter

4 cups mixed vegetables, such
as zucchini, carrots, leeks, and
mushrooms, cut into bite-
size pieces (about 2 lb)

4 medium potatoes (about 1 lb),
peeled and cut into chunks

⅓ cup plus 1 tablespoon
all-purpose flour

2½ cups milk

2 teaspoons Dijon mustard
(optional)

2 cups shredded sharp
cheddar cheese

salt and pepper

- Melt half the butter in a large, heavy casserole or saucepan and gently cook the mixed vegetables for about 20 minutes, stirring occasionally, until tender and golden.

- Cook the potatoes in a large saucepan of lightly salted boiling water for 10–12 minutes, until just tender.

- Meanwhile, place the remaining butter, the flour, and the milk in a saucepan over medium heat, and stir continuously with a balloon whisk or wooden spoon until thickened. Simmer gently for 1–2 minutes, then stir in the Dijon mustard, if using, and half the shredded cheese. Season lightly and set aside.

- Transfer the cooked vegetables to a large ovenproof dish and pour the cheese sauce over them. Sprinkle with the remaining cheese and cook under a preheated broiler for 5–7 minutes, until bubbling and golden. Serve immediately.

---

1 **Quick Vegetable Gratin** Melt
4 tablespoons butter in a saucepan and cook 2 (16 oz) packages frozen mixed vegetables for 3–4 minutes, stirring occasionally. Meanwhile, make the cheese sauce using 3 tablespoons flour, 2 tablespoons butter, and 1¼ cups milk. Simmer for 1–2 minutes, then stir in 1 teaspoon mustard and 1 cup shredded cheddar cheese. Divide the mixture among 4 individual ovenproof dishes, pour the cheese sauce over them, and cook under a hot broiler for 2–3 minutes, until just bubbling and golden. Serve with crusty bread.

2 **Chunky Vegetable Soup with Cheese Croutons** Cook 4 cups finely chopped mixed vegetables, such as zucchini, carrots, leeks, and mushrooms (about 2 lb), in 4 tablespoons butter with 2 chopped garlic cloves for 7–8 minutes, until lightly golden. Add 4 cups hot vegetable stock, season, and simmer for 7–8 minutes, until tender. Meanwhile, sprinkle 1 cup shredded cheddar cheese on 8 slices of baguette and cook under a preheated broiler for 4–5 minutes, until melted and lightly golden. Use a slotted spoon to remove half the vegetables from the pan and set aside. Use a handheld immersion blender to blend the remaining soup, then return the vegetables to the pan and ladle the soup into 4 bowls. Top with the cheesy croutons and serve.

BUD-VEGG-FYF

Vegetable Noodles with Stir-Fry Sauce

Serves 4

1 lb medium dried egg noodles

2 tablespoons vegetable oil

2 carrots, peeled and cut into thin sticks

3½ cups small broccoli florets

4 scallions, cut into ¾-inch lengths

1¼ cups prepared Chinese-style stir-fry sauce

1⅔ cups bean sprouts

2 tablespoons roasted cashew nuts, crushed, to garnish (optional)

- Bring a large saucepan of water to a boil, add the egg noodles, and immediately remove from the heat. Cover and set aside for 4–5 minutes, until tender. Alternatively, cook according to the package directions. Drain and refresh under cold running water.

- Meanwhile, heat the oil in a wok and add the carrots, broccoli, and scallions. Stir-fry gently for 4–5 minutes, until starting to soften.

- Add the stir-fry sauce and heat until bubbling, then add the bean sprouts and drained noodles. Toss until heated through, then serve in 4 large bowls, sprinkled with crushed cashew nuts, if using.

Quick Noodle Salad Cook 1 lb medium dried egg noodles following the main recipe. Peel 2 carrots and cut into thin sticks and thinly slice 4 scallions, then toss the vegetables with the cooled drained noodles and 1½ cups bean sprouts. Make a dressing by combining 2 tablespoons Chinese-style stir-fry sauce, 1 tablespoon light soy sauce, and 3 tablespoons vegetable oil. Toss into the noodles, then mound into 4 bowls and serve sprinkled with 2 tablespoons crushed roasted cashews, if desired.

Aromatic Vegetable and Noodle Soup Cook 1 lb medium dried egg noodles following the main recipe. Heat 1 tablespoon vegetable oil in a large saucepan, and add 4 scallions cut into ¾-inch lengths, 1 tablespoon chopped fresh ginger root, and 2 sliced garlic cloves. Cook gently for 2 minutes, add 5 cups hot vegetable or miso stock, 2 star anise, and 3 tablespoons light soy sauce, and bring to a boil. Simmer gently, uncovered, for about 20 minutes to let the flavors develop, then stir in 2 carrots, peeled and cut into thin sticks, and 3½ cups small broccoli florets. Cook for 2–3 minutes, until just tender. Stir in 1⅔ cups bean sprouts and the noodles for the final minute, then ladle into 4 deep bowls to serve.

QuickCook
Meat and Poultry

Recipes listed by cooking time

30

20

10

30 Pork Meatballs with Couscous

Serves 4

1 onion, coarsely chopped
1 celery stick, coarsely chopped
1⅔ cups button mushrooms
1 large garlic clove, chopped
¼ cup olive oil or vegetable oil
2 cups boiling ham stock or
    vegetable stock
1 (14½ oz) can plum tomatoes
1¼ cups couscous
4 tablespoons butter
1 lb Italian-style link sausages
2 tablespoons chopped parsley
    (optional)

- Place the onion, celery, mushrooms, and garlic in a food processor and pulse until finely chopped. Heat 2 tablespoons of the oil in a large skillet and cook the chopped vegetables for 8 minutes, until lightly golden and tender. Add 1 cup of the stock and the tomatoes to the skillet, and simmer gently for about 18 minutes.

- Place the couscous in a bowl with the butter and pour the remaining stock over it, cover, and set aside for 6–8 minutes, until the grains are tender and all the liquid has been absorbed.

- Meanwhile, remove the skins from the sausages. Roll the meat into 16–20 bite-size meatballs. Heat the remaining oil in a large, nonstick skillet and cook the meatballs for 10–12 minutes, turning frequently, until cooked through.

- Fluff the couscous with a fork, then mound into 4 shallow bowls. Spoon some sauce over the couscous and arrange the meatballs on top. Sprinkle with chopped parsley, if using.

 Quick Sausage and Mushroom Couscous Heat 2 tablespoons oil in a skillet, then cook 1 chopped onion and 1 chopped garlic clove for 4–5 minutes. Add 1½ cups chopped mushrooms and cook for an additional 3 minutes. Add 8 oz sliced, smoked cooked pork sausage and 14s tomato pasta sauce and bring to a boil. Meanwhile, cook 1¼ cups couscous, following the main recipe. Once the sausage is hot, spoon the sauce over the couscous, sprinkle with a handful of chopped parsley, and serve.

 Sausage Stew with Couscous Heat 2 tablespoons olive oil or vegetable oil in a large, deep skillet. Sauté 8 Italian-style link sausages over medium-high heat for 3–4 minutes, until lightly golden. Remove and set aside the sausages and turn down the heat slightly. Add 1 coarsely chopped onion and 1 large chopped garlic clove to the skillet and cook for 4–5 minutes, until softened. Add 1½ cups coarsely chopped mushrooms and cook for 2 minutes, then return the sausages to the skillet. Pour in 1 cup of boiling ham stock or vegetable stock, 1 (14½ oz) can diced tomatoes, and 2 tablespoons tomato paste and simmer for 8–10 minutes, until the sausages are cooked. Cook 1¼ cups couscous, following the main recipe, and serve with the sausages and sauce.

BUD-MEAT-LUH

 # Ginger and Cilantro Turkey Burgers

Serves 4

1 lb ground turkey

1 tablespoon finely grated fresh
  ginger root

3 tablespoons finely chopped
  fresh cilantro

1 cup fresh bread crumbs

2 teaspoons dark soy sauce

2 tablespoons lightly beaten egg

2 tablespoons vegetable oil

black pepper

To serve

¼ cup Mexican salsa

4 large or 8 small hamburger
  buns, sliced and toasted

4–8 lettuce leaves

- Place the turkey in a large bowl with the ginger, cilantro, bread crumbs, and soy sauce. Season with black pepper and add the egg, mixing well to combine. Form into 4 large or 8 small patties.

- Heat the oil in a large, nonstick skillet and sauté the patties for 3–4 minutes on each side, until cooked through and golden.

- Spread the Mexican salsa onto the bottom halves of the toasted buns and top with the lettuce. Place a burger on top of each and cover with the lid. Serve immediately.

 Grilled Turkey with Ginger and Cilantro Dressing Rub 1 tablespoon vegetable oil over 1 lb turkey cutlets. Season with salt and pepper, then heat a ridged grill pan and cook the turkey cutlets for 2–3 minutes on each side, until cooked through and lightly charred. Set aside to cool slightly, then cut into strips. Meanwhile, make a dressing by combining 3 tablespoons vegetable oil with 1 teaspoon grated fresh ginger root, 1 tablespoon Mexican salsa, 2 teaspoons light soy sauce, and 1 tablespoon lime juice. Toss 1 (6 oz) package mixed salad greens with 3 tablespoons finely chopped fresh cilantro and mound into 4 bowls. Divide the turkey strips among the bowls, then drizzle with the dressing and serve with bread rolls, if desired.

 Baked Turkey Cutlets with Ginger and Cilantro Combine 1 tablespoon finely grated fresh ginger root, 3 tablespoons finely chopped fresh cilantro, 2 tablespoons Mexican salsa, and 1 tablespoon light soy sauce. Cut some slashes in 4 turkey cutlets (about 5 oz each) and rub in the ginger and cilantro marinade. Place in an ovenproof dish and cover with foil. Cook in a preheated oven, at 400°F, for about 20 minutes, until cooked through. Serve with 4 cups freshly cooked rice, extra Mexican salsa, and lime wedges.

Breaded Pork Chops with Feta and Lima Bean Salad

Serves 4

4 boneless pork chops
  (about 5 oz each)
2 medium eggs, lightly beaten
3 tablespoons seasoned flour
1½ teaspoons dried oregano
grated rind and juice of 1 lemon
2 cups fresh bread crumbs
¼ cup olive oil or vegetable oil
1⅓ cups diced feta cheese
¾ cup pitted olives
2 large tomatoes, diced
1 (15 oz) can lima beans, drained
  and rinsed
salt and pepper

- Place the pork chops, one at a time, between 2 large pieces of plastic wrap and beat with a rolling pin until about ½ inch thick.

- Put the eggs in a large, shallow bowl and put the seasoned flour on a plate. Stir 1 teaspoon of the dried oregano and the lemon rind into the bread crumbs, season with salt and pepper, and spread out on a separate plate.

- Coat the pork chops on both sides in the seasoned flour, then the egg, and finally the bread crumb mixture.

- Heat half the oil in a large, nonstick skillet and cook the breaded pork chops for 3–4 minutes on each side, until crispy, golden, and cooked through.

- Meanwhile, mix the feta and olives with the diced tomatoes and lima beans. Whisk together the lemon juice with the remaining oil and oregano, and season. Fold into the salad, then spoon onto 4 plates and serve with the pork chops.

 Pork, Feta, and Lima Bean Pockets

Heat ¼ cup oil in a skillet and cook 1 lb pork strips for 4–5 minutes. Meanwhile, arrange 4 flour tortillas on 4 warm plates and top with 3 cups salad greens. Divide 1 (15 oz) can lima beans, drained, rinsed, and warmed, 2 large diced tomatoes, ¾ cup pitted olives, 1⅓ cups diced feta cheese, and 1 teaspoon dried oregano among the tortillas. Top with the pork and squeeze some lemon juice over the mixture. Fold in the sides of the tortillas, then turn to serve.

Feta-Stuffed Pork with Lima Beans

Mix 1 cup bread crumbs with 1 seeded and diced tomato, ¼ cup pitted olives, ⅔ cup crumbled feta cheese, the grated rind of 1 lemon, and 1½ teaspoons dried oregano. Cut slits into the sides of 4 thick, boneless pork chops to make pockets and fill with the prepared mixture. Place on a greased baking sheet, then drizzle with 2 tablespoons of olive oil and the juice of 1 lemon, and roast in a preheated oven, at 400°F, for 20–25 minutes, until cooked and lightly golden. Meanwhile, warm 1 (15 oz) can lima beans, rinsed and drained, in a saucepan with 1 seeded and diced tomato and ½ cup pitted olives, then season with salt and pepper. Spoon onto 4 plates and serve with the pork chops and their juices.

3 Indian-Style Lamb and Peas with Mango Chutney

Serves 4

2 tablespoons vegetable oil
1 large onion, chopped
2 garlic cloves, sliced
¾-inch piece of fresh ginger root, finely chopped
1 green chile, seeded and finely chopped
1 inch cinnamon stick
2–3 cardamom pods, crushed
1 teaspoon ground coriander
1 teaspoon ground cumin
½ teaspoon ground turmeric
½ teaspoon garam masala
1 lb ground lamb
1 cup frozen peas
2 tomatoes, chopped
1 cup boiling water
salt and pepper

To serve

¼ cup mango chutney
chapattis, naans, or boiled rice

- Heat the oil in a large, deep skillet. Add the onion and cook for 3–4 minutes, then add the garlic, ginger, and chile and cook for an additional 2–3 minutes, until golden.

- Stir in the spices, then increase the heat and add the ground lamb. Cook for 2–3 minutes, until browned all over.

- Stir in the peas, tomatoes, and plenty of seasoning, then pour in the measured boiling water. Bring to a boil, reduce the heat, and simmer gently for about 15 minutes, until cooked and thickened. Serve hot with mango chutney and chapattis, naans, or boiled rice.

1 Indian-Style Lamb Chops

Mix together 1 teaspoon ground coriander, 1 teaspoon ground cumin, ½ teaspoon ground turmeric, ½ teaspoon garam masala, and 1 tablespoon vegetable oil. Rub over 8 lamb chops (about 1 lb in total). Cook on a foil-lined broiler rack under a preheated hot broiler for 5–8 minutes, turning once. Set aside for 1–2 minutes, then serve with mango chutney and chapattis, naans, or boiled rice.

2 Quick Lamb Curry

Heat 2 tablespoons vegetable oil in a large skillet, add 3 tablespoons madras curry paste, and cook for 1 minute. Add 1 lb ground lamb and cook for 2–3 minutes, until browned all over. Stir in 1 cup frozen peas and 2 chopped tomatoes, season with salt and pepper, then pour in 1 cup boiling water. Bring to a boil, reduce the heat, and simmer gently for about 15 minutes, until cooked and thickened. Serve hot with mango chutney and chapattis, naans, or boiled rice.

10 Chorizo and Lima Bean Salad

Serves 4

2 tablespoons olive oil or vegetable oil

1 red onion, finely sliced

4 oz chorizo, sliced

1 teaspoon paprika

2 (15 oz) cans lima beans, drained and rinsed

3 tablespoons coarsely chopped parsley

2 tablespoons sherry or red wine vinegar

3 ripe tomatoes, chopped

salt and pepper

- Heat the oil in a large skillet and cook the onion over medium-high heat for 2–3 minutes, until starting to turn golden. Add the chorizo and cook for 1–2 minutes, until golden. Stir in the paprika and lima beans and cook for an additional 1–2 minutes.

- Add the parsley, vinegar, and chopped tomatoes to the skillet, toss well, then remove from the heat. Season with salt and pepper and spoon into 4 shallow bowls to serve.

 Warm Chorizo and Fava Bean Salad

Cook 3⅓ cups frozen fava beans in a large saucepan of lightly salted boiling water for 3–4 minutes, until tender. Drain, refresh under cold running water, then remove the skins from the beans. Follow the main recipe, replacing the lima beans with the fava beans.

 Chorizo and Fava Bean Gratin

Follow the 20-minute recipe, then transfer the beans and sauce to an ovenproof dish. Mix 2 cups fresh bread crumbs with 3 tablespoons grated Parmesan-style cheese and 3 tablespoons coarsely chopped parsley. Sprinkle the mixture over the beans, drizzle with 1 tablespoon oil, and cook under a preheated boiler for 7–8 minutes, until crisp and golden. Serve with a salad.

Pork, Mushroom, and Lemon Tagliatelle

Serves 4

1 lb tagliatelle pasta

2 tablespoons olive oil or vegetable oil

10 oz pork tenderloin, cut into thin strips

10 oz portobello mushrooms, sliced

½ cup dry white wine

1 teaspoon dried tarragon

1 cup heavy cream

salt and pepper

1 lemon, sliced, to garnish

- Cook the tagliatelle in a large saucepan of lightly salted boiling water according to the package directions, until al dente.

- Meanwhile, heat the oil in a deep skillet and sauté the pork strips for 6–7 minutes, until golden. Remove with a slotted spoon and set aside in a bowl.

- Add the mushrooms to the skillet and cook for 3–4 minutes, until soft and golden. Remove and add to the pork.

- If using the lemon, arrange the slices in a single layer in the skillet and cook for 2–3 minutes, turning once, until golden. Remove and set aside.

- Pour the wine and tarragon into the skillet, and let simmer to reduce by half. Return the mushroom and pork to the skillet and pour in the cream. Season well. Simmer gently for 2–3 minutes, until thickened slightly, then serve immediately alongside the tagliatelle, garnished with the lemon slices.

 Pancetta and Mushroom Tagliatelle Cook 1 lb quick-cook tagliatelle according to the package directions. Heat 2 tablespoons oil in a skillet and cook 8 oz chopped pancetta for 3–4 minutes. Add 10 oz sliced portobello mushrooms and cook for 3–4 minutes. Stir in 2 teaspoons chopped fresh tarragon and 1¼ cups light cream, then season and bring to a boil. Stir in 1 tablespoon lemon juice and serve with the tagliatelle.

 Creamy Pork and Mushroom Stroganoff Cook 1 lb tagliatelle according to the package directions. Meanwhile, heat 2 tablespoons olive oil or vegetable oil in a large skillet and cook 1 lb pork strips for 4–5 minutes, until cooked and golden. Remove with a slotted spoon and set aside. Return the skillet to the heat, add 1 sliced onion and 2 chopped garlic cloves, and cook gently for 7–8 minutes, until softened and lightly golden. Add 10 oz sliced portobello mushrooms and sauté gently for an additional 5–6 minutes. Stir in 2 teaspoons paprika, cook for 1 minute, then add 1¼ cups sour cream and bring to a gentle simmer. Season to taste, then return the pork and any juices to the skillet for 1–2 minutes, until hot. Stir in 2 teaspoons lemon juice and 2 tablespoons chopped parsley and serve immediately with the tagliatelle.

3️⃣0️⃣ Marinated Beef Chow Mein with Broccoli

Serves 4

10 oz top sirloin steak,
   cut into strips
1 tablespoon dark soy sauce
3 tablespoons Chinese rice wine
   or dry sherry
1 teaspoon Chinese five-spice
   powder
2 tablespoons cornstarch
½ teaspoon sugar
8 oz medium dried egg noodles
3 tablespoons vegetable oil
1 onion, halved and thinly sliced
1 red bell pepper, cored, seeded,
   and thinly sliced
3½ cups small broccoli florets
2 garlic cloves, thinly sliced
1-inch piece of fresh ginger root,
   cut into matchsticks
¼ cup oyster sauce
½ cup water

- Mix the beef with the soy sauce, rice wine, five-spice powder, cornstarch, and sugar, and set aside to marinate for 15–20 minutes.

- Bring a large saucepan of water to a boil, add the egg noodles, and immediately remove from the heat. Cover and set aside for 4–5 minutes, until tender. Alternatively, cook according to the package directions. Drain and cool under running water. Drain well, then toss with 1 tablespoon of the oil.

- Heat the remaining oil in a large wok or skillet, and stir-fry the onion and bell pepper for 2–3 minutes, until softened slightly, then stir in the broccoli florets and cook for an additional 2–3 minutes. Add the garlic and ginger and cook for 1 minute, stirring frequently.

- Transfer the beef and its marinade to the wok and stir-fry for 3–4 minutes, until well browned. Pour in the oyster sauce and measured water, then add the noodles. Simmer gently for 2–3 minutes, until the noodles are hot. Mound into shallow bowls and serve immediately.

 Beef and Vegetable Chow Mein Heat 3 tablespoons vegetable oil in a wok, add 10 oz top sirloin steak, cut into strips, and cook for 1–2 minutes, until just browned. Add 1 (16 oz) package mixed stir-fry vegetables and cook for 3–4 minutes, until beginning to soften. Stir in 1 lb straight-to-wok egg noodles and 1½ cups Chinese chow mein sauce and cook for 2–3 minutes. Serve in bowls.

2️⃣0️⃣ Beef and Black Bean Chow Mein with Bok choy Cook 8 oz medium dried egg noodles following the main recipe. Heat 2 tablespoons vegetable oil in a large wok or skillet and add 10 oz top sirloin steak, cut into strips. Cook for 2–3 minutes, stirring frequently, until sealed and almost cooked. Remove with a slotted spoon and set aside. Add 3 sliced scallions and 1 sliced yellow bell pepper to the wok and cook for 2–3 minutes, then stir in 8 oz thickly sliced bok choy and cook for an additional 2–3 minutes. Add the garlic and ginger and cook for 1 minute, stirring frequently, then add 1½ cups Chinese black bean sauce and simmer for 2 minutes before returning the beef and noodles to the wok. Cook for 1–2 minutes, until hot, then mound into bowls to serve.

Macaroni and Cheese with Bacon

Serves 4

10 oz macaroni pasta
2 tablespoons olive oil or
   vegetable oil
5 oz smoked bacon, chopped
1½ cups sliced or chopped
   button mushrooms
2 cups milk
⅓ cup plus 1 tablespoon
   all-purpose flour
4 tablespoon butter
1¼ cups shredded medium or
   sharp cheddar cheese
pinch of ground nutmeg
   (optional)
freshly ground black pepper

- Cook the macaroni in a large saucepan of lightly salted boiling water for 8–10 minutes, or according to the package directions, until al dente.

- Meanwhile, heat the oil in a skillet and cook the bacon for 3–4 minutes, until cooked and lightly golden. Add the mushrooms and cook for an additional 3–4 minutes, until softened. Remove from the heat and set aside.

- Pour the milk into a saucepan with the flour and butter, and cook over medium heat, beating continuously, until thickened and simmering gently. Cook for 2–3 minutes, then remove from the heat and stir in half the shredded cheese.

- Drain the pasta and combine with the cheese sauce, bacon, and mushrooms. Add the nutmeg, if using, and season with black pepper. Transfer to a large ovenproof dish, sprinkle with the remaining cheese, and cook under a preheated broiler for 5–6 minutes, until golden and bubbling, and serve.

 Cheesy Mushroom and Ham Macaroni

Cook 1 lb quick-cook macaroni according to the package directions. Meanwhile, heat 2 tablespoons oil in a deep skillet and cook 1½ cups sliced button mushrooms for 3–4 minutes, until softened. Add 1¼ cups heavy cream, 5 oz chopped ham, 1¼ cups shredded medium or sharp cheddar cheese, a pinch of ground nutmeg, and seasoning, then heat until bubbling gently. Drain the pasta, stir into the sauce, and serve immediately.

 Baked Cheese and Ham Macaroni

Cook 2 (9 oz) packages spinach and ricotta-filled pasta in a large saucepan of lightly salted boiling water according to the package directions, until not quite tender. Meanwhile, make the cheese sauce following the main recipe. Stir 5 oz chopped ham and 2 (4 oz) cans mushrooms pieces and stems, drained, into the cheese sauce, then stir into the pasta. Transfer to a large ovenproof dish, sprinkle with the remaining cheese, and bake in a preheated oven, at 375°F, for about 20 minutes, until bubbling and golden. Serve with a crunchy green salad.

Fried Steak with Green Peppercorn Sauce

Serves 4

2 tablespoons olive oil

4 skirt steaks (about 4 oz each)

2 tablespoons butter

½ cup light cream

2 teaspoons green peppercorns
in water, drained

salt and pepper

To serve

green salad

crusty bread or French fries

- Heat the oil in a large, nonstick skillet and sauté the steaks for 1–3 minutes on each side, depending on how you like your steak. Season with salt and pepper, remove the steaks from the skillet, and transfer to a warm ovenproof dish to let rest for a few minutes.

- Add the butter, cream, and peppercorns to the skillet, and simmer over medium-low heat for 1–2 minutes, scraping the bottom of the skillet to loosen any tasty sediment.

- Serve the steaks drizzled with the sauce, accompanied by a green salad and bread or French fries.

 Green Peppercorn Burgers with Blue Cheese Sauce Place 1 lb ground beef in a bowl with 1 chopped red onion, 2 teaspoons green peppercorns in water, drained, ¼ cup dried bread crumbs, 1 beaten egg, and 1 tablespoon finely chopped parsley or chives, then season and mix to combine. Form into 4 patties, then heat 2 tablespoons olive oil in a skillet and cook for 4–5 minutes on each side, until cooked through. Meanwhile, place 4 oz creamy blue cheese in a small bowl with 2 tablespoons crème fraîche and plenty of black pepper. Mash together until smooth and serve on buns with the burgers and some slices of fresh tomato.

 Beef and Green Peppercorn Goulash Heat 2 tablespoons olive oil in a large, nonstick skillet and add 1 lb sliced top tenderloin steak. Cook over medium-high heat for 3–4 minutes, until browned all over, then remove with a slotted spoon and set aside. Reduce the heat slightly and add 1 extra tablespoon of oil, then cook 1 sliced onion, 1 sliced red or green bell pepper, and 2 chopped garlic cloves for 6–7 minutes, until softened and lightly golden. Stir in 1 tablespoon all-purpose flour and 1 tablespoon paprika, cook for 1 minute, then add 1 (14½ oz) can diced tomatoes, 1 tablespoon tomato paste, 1¼ cups hot beef stock or vegetable stock, 2 teaspoons green peppercorns in water, drained, and seasoning to taste. Bring to a boil and simmer gently for 15–18 minutes, until rich and thick. Return the beef to the skillet with any juices and stir to heat through. Stir in ½ cup light cream and serve with boiled rice and chopped parsley, to garnish.

BUD-MEAT-BAA

30 Baked Chicken with Lime

Serves 4

2 limes
1-inch piece of fresh ginger root, peeled and finely grated
1 teaspoon Thai fish sauce
1 tablespoon peanut oil or vegetable oil
1 large bunch of cilantro
4 chicken breasts (about 5 oz each)
2 cups jasmine rice, rinsed
2¾ cups cold water
salt

- Preheat the oven to 400°F and line a roasting pan with foil. Finely grate the rind from the 2 limes, squeeze the juice from one of them, and finely slice the other.

- Place the lime rind and juice in a mini chopper or the small bowl of a food processor with the ginger, fish sauce, oil, and cilantro, including the stems. Blend to make a paste.

- Cut 3 deep slashes diagonally into the chicken breasts and rub the paste all over the chicken. Place a slice of lime into each slash.

- Place the chicken breasts in the roasting pan, cover with foil, and bake in the preheated oven for 18–20 minutes, until the chicken is cooked through.

- Meanwhile, place the rice in a large saucepan with the measured water, season with salt, and bring to a boil. Reduce the heat, cover with a tight-fitting lid, and cook gently according to the package directions, until all of the water has been absorbed and the rice is tender and sticky. Serve the chicken with the sticky rice, drizzled with chicken juices.

 Chicken and Lime Noodle Salad Place 1 lb rice noodles, cooked and cooled, into a bowl with 2 cups cooked chicken strips, the grated rind of 1 lime, 1 bunch of cilantro, chopped, and 1 thinly sliced red bell pepper and toss to combine. Pour 3 tablespoons vegetable oil into a small mixing bowl with 2 tablespoons lime juice, 2 teaspoons grated ginger, and 1 tablespoon Thai fish sauce, and whisk to combine. Drizzle the salad with the dressing to serve.

 Chicken and Lime Stir-Fry Cook 2 cups jasmine rice following the main recipe. Meanwhile, heat 1 tablespoon peanut oil or vegetable oil in a large, nonstick skillet and add 1 lb boneless, skinless chicken thigh, sliced. Stir-fry for 7–8 minutes, until cooked and golden, then add 1 sliced red bell pepper, 1 tablespoon chopped ginger, and 3 thickly sliced scallions. Stir-fry for an additional 3–4 minutes, until softened.

Mix together 2 tablespoons honey, 2 tablespoons light soy sauce, 1 teaspoon sesame oil, and 2 tablespoons lime juice. Stir this sauce into the skillet, cook for 30 seconds, then spoon over the cooked rice to serve.

10 Warm Tomato, Liver, and Bacon Salad

Serves 4

2 tablespoons olive oil
4 oz smoked bacon, chopped
8 oz chicken livers, trimmed
4 ripe tomatoes, sliced
4 oz watercress or mache
½ red onion, halved and sliced
salt and pepper

For the dressing

3 tablespoons olive oil
1 tablespoon red wine vinegar
1 teaspoon Dijon mustard
pinch of sugar

- Heat the oil in a nonstick skillet and cook the bacon for 3–4 minutes, until crisp and golden. Remove from the skillet with a slotted spoon and set aside. Season the chicken livers with salt and pepper and add to the hot skillet. Cook for 4–5 minutes, until browned and cooked through.

- Combine all the dressing ingredients in a jar with a tight-fitting lid and shake well.

- Arrange the tomatoes on 4 plates with the watercress and red onion. Divde the liver and bacon among the prepared salads and serve immediately, drizzled with the dressing.

 Liver and Bacon Tagliatelle Cook 1 lb tagliatelle according to the package directions. Meanwhile, heat 2 tablespoons oil in a skillet and cook 4 oz chopped smoked bacon for 3–4 minutes. Add 1 chopped red onion and 2 chopped garlic cloves. Cook for 4–5 minutes. Add 8 oz chicken livers, trimmed, and sauté for 2–3 minutes to brown, then add 2 tablespoons dry sherry, scraping the bottom of the skillet to loosen any sediment. Add 1 cup light cream, 4 chopped sun-dried tomatoes, and 1 teaspoon dried sage. Season and simmer for 2–3 minutes, until the livers are just cooked. Serve with the tagliatelle.

 Crispy Potatoes with Liver and Bacon Cook 12 small new potatoes (about 1 lb) in a saucepan of lightly salted boiling water for about 10 minutes, until almost tender. Drain well, toss with 2 tablespoons oil, then transfer to a roasting pan and cook in a preheated oven, at 425°F, for 15–20 minutes, shaking occasionally, until crisp and golden. Meanwhile, cook 4 oz chopped smoked bacon, 1 chopped red onion, 2 chopped garlic cloves, and 8 oz chicken livers, following the 20-minute recipe. Once the chicken livers are brown, sprinkle 1 tablespoon all-purpose flour into the skillet with 1 tablespoon tomato paste, cook for 1 minute, then add 2 tablespoons Madeira, if desired, followed by ⅔ cup hot chicken stock. Simmer gently for 3–4 minutes, until the sauce has thickened slightly and the livers are just cooked through. Remove from the heat, stir the cooked potatoes and 2 teaspoons chopped sage leaves into the skillet, then season to taste and spoon into 4 shallow dishes. Serve immediately with the watercress and tomatoes.

30 Beef Casseroles with Crunchy Topping

Serves 4

4 medium floury potatoes
(about 1 lb), such as russets,
peeled and cut into chunks
2 tablespoons olive oil
1 lb top sirloin steak, sliced
2 garlic cloves, chopped
1 leek, sliced
5 cups quartered mushrooms
6 tablespoons butter
2 teaspoons paprika
1 tablespoon tomato paste
½ cup heavy cream
1 beef bouillon cube
⅔ cup water
1 cup fresh bread crumbs
2 tablespoons chopped chives
1 cup shredded cheddar cheese
salt and pepper

- Cook the potatoes in a large saucepan of lightly salted boiling water for 12–15 minutes, until tender.

- Meanwhile, heat the oil in a large skillet and cook the steak for 3–4 minutes, until browned all over, then remove from the skillet and set aside. Add the garlic, leek, and mushrooms to the skillet with 2 tablespoons of the butter and cook for 7–8 minutes. Stir in the paprika and tomato paste, followed by the cream, bouillon cube, and measured water. Bring to a boil and simmer gently for 5–6 minutes to thicken slightly.

- Drain the potatoes and return to the pan over low heat to remove excess moisture. Turn off the heat, then mash the potatoes until smooth with the remaining butter. Season. Mix the bread crumbs with the chives and cheddar. Stir the beef and any juices back into the mushrooms, then divide among 4 individual casseroles. Top each casserole with mashed potatoes, then the topping. Cook under a preheated broiler for 5–6 minutes, until bubbling, golden, and crunchy. Serve hot.

---

10 Steaks with Crunchy-Topped Mashed Potatoes

Mix 1 cup fresh bread crumbs with 2 tablespoons chopped chives and 1 cup shredded cheddar. Place 1 (24 oz) package mashed potato in a small casserole and sprinkle over the topping. Cook under a preheated broiler for 5–6 minutes. Meanwhile, heat a ridged grill pan. Rub 1 tablespoon oil over 4 skirt steaks (about 4 oz each), and cook for 1–3 minutes on each side. Serve with the crunchy-topped mashed potatoes and broccoli.

20 Quick Corned Beef Casseroles

Heat 1 tablespoon olive oil and 2 tablespoons butter in a large saucepan, add 3 cups chopped mushrooms with 2 chopped garlic cloves and 1 sliced leek, and cook for 7–8 minutes, until softened and lightly golden. Mix 1 cup fresh bread crumbs in a bowl with 2 tablespoons chopped chives and 1 cup shredded cheddar cheese. Stir in 1 (15 oz) can baked beans and 1 lb crumbled corned beef into the mushroom mixture and heat through thoroughly.

Transfer to an ovenproof dish and top with 1 (24 oz) package warm mashed potatoes. Sprinkle the bread crumb topping over the top and cook under a preheated broiler for 5–6 minutes, until golden and crunchy. Serve with broccoli.

Sausages with Mashed Potatoes and Celeriac

Serves 4

5 medium floury potatoes
(about 1¼ lb), such as russets,
peeled and diced
1 small celeriac, peeled and diced
8 Italian-style link sausages
4 tablespoons butter
1 tablespoon chopped thyme
leaves
salt and pepper
steamed carrots, to serve

- Cook the potatoes and celeriac in a large saucepan of lightly salted boiling water for about 15 minutes, until tender. Drain, then return to the pan and place over low heat for 30 seconds to remove excess liquid.

- Meanwhile, cook the sausages under a preheated broiler for 12–15 minutes, turning occasionally, until cooked and golden.

- Mash the potato and celeriac with the butter, thyme, and plenty of seasoning. Serve the broiled sausages with the mashed potatoes and celeriac and some steamed carrots.

Sausages with Celeriac Remoulade

Heat 1 tablespoon olive oil or vegetable oil in a skillet and cook 12 small pork sausages or cocktail franks for about 8 minutes, turning occasionally, until cooked through and golden. Meanwhile, shred 1 small peeled celeriac and toss with 1 tablespoon lemon juice. Add ⅓ cup mayonnaise, 2 tablespoons whole-grain mustard, and a pinch of sugar, season with salt and pepper, and mix well to combine. Spoon onto plates and serve with the cooked sausages.

Potato and Celeriac Soup with Sausage Croutons

Melt the butter in a large saucepan with 1 tablespoon oil and add 1 chopped onion and 2 chopped garlic cloves. Cook for 6–7 minutes, until softened and lightly golden. Add 1 small diced celeriac and 3 medium potatoes, diced, and cook for 3–4 minutes, until lightly golden. Stir in 5 cups hot vegetable stock and most of 1 tablespoon chopped thyme leaves, reserving 1 teaspoon to garnish. Season and bring to a boil, then reduce the heat and simmer gently for about 15 minutes, until the celeriac and potatoes are tender. Meanwhile, heat 1 tablespoon oil in a skillet and cook 4 chopped Italian-style link sausages for 8–10 minutes, until crisp and golden. Drain on paper towels and set aside. Blend the soup using a handheld immersion blender and ladle into bowls. Sprinkle with the crispy sausage pieces and the remaining thyme to serve.

30 Creamy Cider Chicken with Rice

Serves 4

3 tablespoons olive oil or
   vegetable oil
8 boneless chicken thighs
   (about 1¼ lb in total)
2–3 tablespoons seasoned flour
4 oz bacon, chopped
1½ cups sliced mushrooms
1 cup boiling vegetable stock
   or chicken stock
1 cup dry cider
2 tablespoons cider vinegar
2 cups long-grain rice
¼ cup light cream or
   crème fraîche
salt and pepper

- Heat 2 tablespoons of the oil in a large, deep skillet. Dust the chicken with the seasoned flour and cook in the skillet, skin side down, for about 10 minutes, until golden and crisp.

- Meanwhile, heat the remaining oil in a small skillet and cook the bacon for 3–4 minutes, until golden. Add the mushrooms and cook for an additional 2–3 minutes, until softened.

- Turn over the chicken thighs, then add the bacon and mushrooms to the skillet. Pour the stock, cider, and cider vinegar over the chicken, bring to a boil, then reduce the heat and simmer gently for about 15 minutes, until the chicken thighs are cooked.

- Meanwhile, cook the rice according to the package directions, then drain and divide among 4 shallow dishes.

- Arrange the chicken thighs alongside the rice, then stir the cream into the skillet. Season with salt and pepper, then spoon the sauce over the chicken to serve.

Creamy Chicken Rice

Heat 2 tablespoons oil in a skillet and cook 4 oz chopped bacon for 3–4 minutes, until golden. Add 1½ cups sliced mushrooms and cook for an additional 2–3 minutes. Add 2 cups diced, cooked chicken, 3 cups cooked rice, and 1¼ cups crème fraîche, then season well and stir over the heat for 1–2 minutes, until hot. Spoon the creamy rice into 4 bowls to serve.

Quick Creamy Cider Chicken

For a quicker version of the main recipe, remove the skin and slice 8 boneless chicken thighs. Heat 2 tablespoons oil in a large saucepan and cook the chicken for 5–6 minutes, until golden. Meanwhile, cook 2 cups quick-cooking long-grain rice in a large saucepan of lightly salted boiling water according to the package directions. Add 4 oz chopped bacon to the chicken and cook for 3–4 minutes, then stir in 1½ cups sliced mushrooms and cook for an additional 2–3 minutes. Pour in 1 cup dry cider and 1 tablespoon cider vinegar and simmer gently for 7–8 minutes, until the chicken is cooked and the cider has reduced slightly. Remove from the heat, pour in ¼ cup light cream or crème fraîche, season with salt and pepper, and serve spooned over the cooked rice.

30 Lamb Stew with Mashed Potatoes

Serves 4

1 onion, coarsely chopped
1 large carrot, coarsely chopped
1 celery stick, coarsely chopped
2 garlic cloves
2 tablespoons vegetable oil
1 lb ground lamb
2 tablespoons all-purpose flour
2 cups hot lamb stock or
   vegetable stock
1 (14½ oz) can diced tomatoes
1 tablespoon ketchup
1 tablespoon Worcestershire
   sauce
2–3 bay leaves (optional)
8 medium floury potatoes
   (about 2 lb), such as russets,
   peeled and coarsely diced
4 tablespoons butter
3–4 tablespoons milk
salt and pepper

- Place the onion, carrot, celery, and garlic in a food processor and pulse quickly until finely chopped. Heat the oil in a large, deep skillet or casserole and cook the chopped vegetables for about 8 minutes, until tender and lightly golden. Add the meat and cook over high heat, stirring occasionally, for 2–3 minutes, until browned all over.

- Sprinkle with the flour and stir well. Pour in the stock, then add the diced tomatoes, ketchup, Worcestershire sauce, bay leaves, if using, and plenty of seasoning. Bring to a boil, then reduce the heat slightly, cover, and simmer for 15–18 minutes, until thickened.

- Meanwhile, cook the potatoes in a large saucepan of lightly salted boiling water for about 15 minutes, until tender. Drain the potatoes, return them to the pan with the butter, and mash until smooth over low heat. Stir in the milk and season with salt and pepper.

- Remove and discard the bay leaves, spoon the meat mixture into bowls, and serve with the mashed potatoes.

 ### Lamb Cutlets with Couscous

Rub 1 tablespoon olive oil over 4 lamb cutlets (about 4 oz each). Sprinkle with 1 teaspoon dried rosemary and a pinch of salt and pepper. Heat a nonstick skillet and cook the lamb cutlets for 2–4 minutes each side, depending on how you like your lamb. Meanwhile, pour 1¼ cups boiling water over 1¼ cup seasoned couscous mix, preferably Mediterranean flavor, then cover and set aside for 5–8 minutes, or prepare according to the package directions, until the liquid has been absorbed and the grains are tender. Spoon the couscous onto 4 warm plates and serve with the lamb cutlets and lemon wedges.

 ### Fast Lamb Casserole Heat

2 tablespoons vegetable oil in a skillet and sauté 1 lb ground lamb for 7–8 minutes, until browned, then add 1 (16 oz) jar chunky vegetable pasta sauce. Simmer for 3–4 minutes, then pour into a casserole and top with 1 (24 oz) package warm mashed potatoes. Sprinkle with 1 cup shredded cheddar cheese and cook under a preheated broiler for 6–7 minutes, until golden.

BUD-MEAT-SAD

1 Cajun-Spiced Hot Dogs

Serves 4

2 tablespoons vegetable oil
1 red onion, halved and sliced
2 red bell peppers, or 1 red and
  1 yellow bell pepper, cored,
  seeded, and sliced
8 turkey or beef frankfurters
1 tablespoon Cajun seasoning mix

To serve

8 hot dog buns, warmed
store-bought salsa (optional)

- Heat the oil in a large, nonstick skillet and cook the onions and bell peppers over high heat for 6–7 minutes, until slightly charred.

- Reduce the heat slightly and add the frankfurters and Cajun spices. Cook for 2–3 minutes, until hot. Serve the hot dogs and cooked vegetables in warm buns with salsa, if desired.

 Cajun-Spiced Sausage Fajitas Cook 8 Italian-style link sausages under a preheated broiler for 12 minutes, turning frequently, until cooked through and golden. Meanwhile, heat 2 tablespoons vegetable oil in a skillet and cook 1 halved and sliced red onion and 2 sliced red bell peppers over high heat for 6–7 minutes, until slightly charred. Thickly slice the sausages diagonally and add to the skillet with 1 tablespoon Cajun seasoning mix, stirring frequently, for 2–3 minutes, until the sausages are golden. Divide the mixture among 4–8 soft flour tortillas. Top with 1¼ cup shredded cheddar cheese, 1 small, shredded iceberg lettuce, and some store-bought salsa. Roll up the tortillas, cut in half, and serve immediately.

 Cajun-Roasted Sausages with Rice and Tortillas Cut 8 Italian-style link sausages into 1½-inch pieces and place in a bowl with 2 diced red bell peppers, 1 diced eggplant, and 1 red onion, cut into thin wedges. Add 3 tablespoons oil and 2 tablespoons Cajun seasoning mix, toss well together, then transfer to a large baking sheet. Cook in a preheated oven, at 450°F, for 20–25 minutes, turning occasionally, until the sausages are cooked and the vegetables slightly softened. Meanwhile, cook 2 cups quick-cooking long-grain rice in a large saucepan of lightly salted boiling water according to the package directions, until just tender.

Serve the Cajun-roasted sausages with the cooked rice, soft flour tortillas, and salsa.

Double Whammy Hamburgers with Pickles

Serves 4

1 lb ground beef
1 onion, finely chopped
1 cup fresh bread crumbs
½ teaspoon dried garlic powder
1 egg, lightly beaten
2 tablespoons olive oil
  or vegetable oil
4 large hamburger buns
4 slices of American cheese
1 cup dill pickle slices
salt and pepper

To serve

4 cups mixed salad greens
barbecue sauce (optional)

· Place the ground beef in a bowl with the onion, bread crumbs, garlic powder, and egg. Season with salt and pepper, mix to combine, then form into 8 flat patties.

· Heat the oil in a large, nonstick skillet and cook the patties for 3–4 minutes on each side, until cooked and golden.

· Arrange mixed salad greens on the bottom half of each hamburger bun and top with some pickle slices, a burger, a slice of cheese, a second burger, barbecue sauce, if desired, and another layer of pickles, before replacing the lids.

 Open Beef Sandwiches Halve a French baguette horizontally and cut each piece in half to create 4 lengths. Toast under a preheated broiler, cut side up, for about 2 minutes, until just golden. Mix 1 tablespoon creamed horseradish with 3 tablespoons mayonnaise and spread on the pieces of bread. Top each with a handful of mixed salad greens and a layer of dill pickle slices. Arrange 4 oz thinly sliced roast beef or corned beef on top, finish with ½ red onion, thinly sliced, and serve immediately.

 Cheesy Corned Beef Hash Parboil 4 medium potatoes (about 1 lb), such as russets, cut into bite-size chunks, in a large saucepan of lightly salted boiling water for 7–8 minutes, then drain. Meanwhile, heat 2 tablespoons olive oil or vegetable oil in a large, nonstick skillet and cook 1 finely chopped onion and 2 chopped garlic cloves for 8–9 minutes, until soft and golden. Crumble 1 lb corned beef into the bottom of a lightly greased casserole and top with the cooked onions. Clean the skillet, then return to the heat with 2 extra tablespoons oil and sauté the potatoes gently for 7–8 minutes, turning frequently, until golden and tender. Arrange 1 cup dill pickle slices and 8 slices of American cheese over the onions and top with the potatoes. Cook in a preheated oven, at 450°F, for 10–12 minutes, until hot and crispy. Meanwhile, poach 4 eggs in a large saucepan of simmering water for 3 minutes. Serve the corned beef hash with the poached eggs and a green salad.

30 Pork Chops with Mashed Parsnips and Apples

Serves 4

2 lb parsnips, peeled and
   cut into chunks
2 cooking apples, peeled, cored,
   and cut into chunks
1 tablespoon olive oil or
   vegetable oil
4 thick pork chops (about
   7 oz each)
1 stick butter
½ cup whole milk or light cream
1 tablespoon chopped sage
pinch of ground nutmeg
4 oz taleggio or mozzarella
   cheese, cut into 8 slices
salt and pepper
steamed green beans, to serve

- Cook the parsnips in a large saucepan of lightly salted boiling water for about 15 minutes, adding the apples after 5 minutes, until both are tender.

- Rub the oil over the pork chops, season well, then cook on a foil-lined broiler rack under a preheated broiler for 15–18 minutes, turning once, until cooked through and golden.

- Drain the parsnips and apples, then return to the pan and place over low heat for 1–2 minutes to remove excess moisture. Remove from the heat and mash well with the butter and milk. Add the sage and nutmeg, season with salt and pepper, and beat until smooth. Keep warm.

- Top each pork chop with 2 slices of cheese, return to the broiler, and cook for 2–3 minutes, until melted and golden.

- Spoon the mashed parsnips and apples onto 4 plates and serve with the pork chops and steamed green beans.

 Bacon, Apple, and Taleggio Toasts Cook 8 bacon slices under a preheated broiler for 5–6 minutes, until crisp and golden. Meanwhile, lightly toast 4 bread slices in a toaster. Spread each slice of toast with 1 tablespoon applesauce, then top with the bacon, followed by 1–2 slices taleggio or mozzarella cheese. Return to the broiler for 2–3 minutes, until melting and golden. Serve immediately with green salad.

 Pork with Caramelized Apples and Mashed Parsnips Cook 4 each medium potatoes and parsnips, peeled and cut into chunks, in a large saucepan of lightly salted boiling water for 12–15 minutes, until tender. Drain, return to the pan, and mash with 4 tablespoons butter, 1 tablespoon chopped sage, and a pinch of ground nutmeg. Meanwhile, core 2 apples, such as Pippin, and cut each into 8 wedges. Heat 4 tablespoons butter in a large, nonstick skillet, add the apple wedges, and cook for 8–10 minutes, until soft and slightly caramelized. Wipe the skillet clean and return to the heat. Add 1 tablespoon olive oil or vegetable oil and cook 4 thin pork cutlets (about 4 oz each), for 4–5 minutes on each side, until golden and cooked through. Spoon the mashed parsnips onto 4 plates, arrange the pork cutlets by the side, and top with the caramelized apples to serve.

30 Turkey Milanese with Garlic Mayonnaise and Garlic Bread

Serves 4

4 turkey cutlets (about 4 oz each)
2 medium eggs, beaten
3 tablespoons seasoned flour
2 cups fresh bread crumbs
2 small garlic cloves, crushed
4 tablespoons butter, softened
2 tablespoons finely chopped
  parsley
1 small French baguette or
  ciabatta loaf
3 tablespoons vegetable oil
salt and pepper
lemon wedge, to garnish
salad greens, to serve

For the garlic mayonnaise

1 large egg yolk
½ teaspoon crushed garlic
1 teaspoon white wine vinegar
½ teaspoon Dijon mustard
⅔ cup vegetable oil

- Place the turkey cutlets, one at a time, between 2 pieces of plastic wrap and beat with a rolling pin until about ½ inch thick. Put the beaten eggs in a large, shallow bowl, and place the seasoned flour and bread crumbs on 2 separate plates. Coat the turkey on both sides in the seasoned flour, followed by the egg, then finally the bread crumbs. Set aside. Preheat the oven to 400°F.

- To make the mayonnaise, put the egg yolk into a mini chopper or the small bowl of a food processor with the ½ teaspoon garlic, vinegar, and mustard, and pulse to combine. Add the oil in a slow, steady stream, blending continuously until the mixture has the consistency of mayonnaise. Season to taste.

- Mash the 2 garlic cloves into the butter with the parsley. Cut slices into the bread loaf, not quite cutting all the way through, then spread the garlic butter onto all the cut sides. Wrap in foil and place in the preheated oven for 5 minutes, then open the foil and cook for an additional 2–3 minutes.

- Meanwhile, heat the oil in a large, nonstick skillet and cook the turkey cutlets for 3–4 minutes on each side, until cooked through. Serve with salad greens, the garlic bread, and garlic mayonnaise and garnish with a lemon wedge.

1 Garlicky Turkey Bagels

Slice and toast 4 bagels and spread the cut sides with 2–4 tablespoons prepared garlic mayonnaise. Place the bottom halves on 4 plates and divide 8 oz) wafer-thin turkey between them. Top each with a slice of American cheese and a handful of salad greens, then add a little thinly sliced red onion. Replace the tops and serve cut in half.

2 Turkey Saltimbocca with Garlic Bread

Beat 4 turkey cutlets to flatten them, following the main recipe. Mash 2 crushed garlic cloves into 4 tablespoons softened butter with 2 tablespoons chopped parsley. Spread the butter over the turket cutlets, then top each with 1 thin slice of prosciutto and secure with toothpicks. Dust each cutlet with seasoned flour. Heat 3 tablespoons oil in a nonstick skillet and cook the turkey for 2–3 minutes each side, until cooled through. Remove from the skillet and place somewhere warm to rest for 1–2 minutes. Meanwhile, pour ½ cup dry white wine into the skillet, scraping the bottom to deglaze, and simmer for 1–2 minutes to reduce. Arrange the turkey on 4 warm plates and drizzle with the juices. Serve with green salad and store-bought garlic bread.

BUD-MEAT-KOP

30 Pork Balls with Sweet-and-Sour Sauce

Serves 4

1 lb ground pork

2 scallions, finely chopped, plus extra to garnish

1 teaspoon crushed garlic

2 teaspoons minced fresh ginger root

1 tablespoon cornstarch

1 small egg white, whisked

3–4 tablespoons vegetable oil or peanut oil

2 cups jasmine rice

soy sauce, to serve (optional)

For the sweet-and-sour sauce

1 (8 oz) can pineapple chunks in juice

½ cup ketchup

2½ tablespoons light brown sugar

2 tablespoons vinegar

2 teaspoons light soy sauce

- Place the ground pork in a large bowl with the scallions, garlic, and ginger. Whisk the cornstarch into the egg white and add to the pork, mixing until well combined. Form the mixture into 20–24 balls. Heat the oil in a large, nonstick skillet. Cook the meatballs for 10–12 minutes, turning occasionally, until cooked through and golden.

- Meanwhile, place the rice in a saucepan with 3 cups of cold water. Bring to a boil, season, cover, and simmer gently for 11–14 minutes, until the rice is tender and the liquid has been absorbed. Garnish with scallions.

- To make the sweet-and-sour sauce, put the pineapple and its juice into a mini chopper or food processor and pulse until crushed but not smooth. Alternatively, chop finely by hand. Pour into a small saucepan with the remaining ingredients, then bring to a boil, reduce the heat, and simmer gently for 5–7 minutes, until thickened.

- Drain the excess oil from the skillet of meatballs, then pour the sauce into the skillet and simmer for a minute or two until well coated. Spoon the meatballs and sauce over the rice and serve immediately with soy sauce, if desired.

10 Sweet-and-Sour Pork Noodles

Heat 2 tablespoons oil in a nonstick skillet and cook 1 lb pork strips for 6–7 minutes, until cooked and golden. Stir in 1 (16 oz) package stir-fry vegetables with sweet-and-sour sauce and heat for 1–2 minutes, until bubbling. Toss the sweet-and-sour pork with 1¼ lb hot straight-to-wok noodles, and mound into bowls to serve.

20 Sweet-and-Sour Pork with Vegetables

Cut 1 lb lean pork into cubes. Place 2 cups jasmine rice in a saucepan with 3 cups cold water, bring to a boil, season with salt, cover, and simmer gently according to the package directions until the rice is tender and the liquid has been absorbed. Heat 2 tablespoons oil in a large, nonstick skillet and cook the pork for 2–3 minutes, until browned. Add 1 sliced onion and 1 sliced red bell pepper and stir-fry for 3–4 minutes, until beginning to soften. Add 1½ cups sliced mushrooms and cook for an additional 3–4 minutes, until softened. Meanwhile, make the sweet-and-sour sauce following the main recipe, then add to the pork and simmer gently for 2–3 minutes, until the pork is cooked through. Serve with the cooked rice.

30 Lamb Skewers with Chickpeas and Rice

Serves 4

2 tablespoons olive oil
   or vegetable oil
1 onion, finely chopped
2 garlic cloves, finely chopped
1 teaspoon ground cumin
1 teaspoon ground coriander
½ teaspoon ground cinnamon
pinch of allspice (optional)
1 cup long-grain rice
1 (15 oz) can chickpeas, drained
   and rinsed
1 lb ground lamb
⅔ cup crumbled feta cheese
1 egg, beaten
1 bunch of cilantro, chopped
salt and pepper
store-bought tzatziki (optional),
   to serve

- Heat the oil in a small skillet and cook the onion for 4–5 minutes. Add the garlic and cook for 3–4 minutes. Add the spices and cook for an additional minute, then remove from the heat and season with black pepper.

- Cook the rice according to package directions until tender.

- Meanwhile, place half the chickpeas in the bowl of a food processor and pulse to chop. Add the lamb and pulse to combine. Scrape into a large bowl and add the feta. Stir in the cooked onions, then add the egg and mix until just combined.

- Form the mixture into 16–20 balls, then thread onto 4 metal skewers and flatten each one gently. Place on a foil-lined broiler rack and cook under a preheated broiler for about 8 minutes, turning once, until cooked through and golden.

- Meanwhile, fold the remaining chickpeas and chopped cilantro into the drained rice and spoon on to 4 plates. Serve with the rice and a spoonful of tzatziki, if using.

---

1 Lamb Skewers with Chickpea Salad

Chop ½ (15 oz) can drained and rinsed chickpeas (reserve the rest of the can) in a food processor with 2 scallions, 1 teaspoon each cumin and coriander, and ½ teaspoon cinnamon. Add 1 lb ground lamb and 1 egg. Season, then pulse. Form into 4 flattened sausages. Sauté in 2 tablespoons oil for 7–8 minutes, turning once. Combine the remaining chickpeas with a bunch of cilantro, chopped, ⅔ cup crumbled feta cheese, 2 tablespoons oil, and 1 tablespoon lemon juice and serve.

2 Lamb Kebabs with Chickpeas

Crush 2 garlic cloves, and mix with 1 teaspoon ground cumin, 1 teaspoon ground coriander, ½ teaspoon ground cinnamon, a pinch of allspice (optional), and 1 tablespoon oil. Rub the mixture all over 1 lb diced lamb or beef. Cut 1 onion and 1 green bell pepper into bite-size pieces, then thread onto 8 short metal skewers with the meat. Place on a foil-lined broiler rack and cook under a preheated broiler for 6–8 minutes, turning occasionally, until cooked but tender. Cook 1 cup long-grain rice in a saucepan of lightly salted boiling water according to package directions, until tender. Fold ½ g (15 oz) can chickpeas, drained and rinsed, and 1 small bunch of cilantro, chopped, into the drained rice, and serve with the kebabs, ⅔ cup crumbled feta cheese, and store-bought tzatziki (optional).

Mustard and Cheese Broiled Ham

Serves 4

1 tablespoon vegetable oil
4 ham steaks (about 6 oz each)
2 tablespoons whole-grain
  mustard
2 tablespoons chopped mixed
  herbs, such as parsley, chives,
  thyme, and oregano
²⁄₃ cup shredded cheddar cheese
2 scallions, finely sliced

To serve

crusty bread
mixed salad greens

- Rub the oil over the ham steaks and arrange on a foil-lined broiler rack. Cook under a preheated broiler for 4–5 minutes on each side, until cooked through.

- Meanwhile, mix the mustard with the chopped herbs, grated cheese, and scallions. Spoon the mixture onto the ham steaks, return to the broiler, and cook under moderate heat for an additional 3–4 minutes, until melted and golden.

- Serve with crusty bread and mixed salad greens.

---

10 Grilled Ham and Cheese with Mustard Sandwiches

Mix 1¼ cups shredded cheddar cheese in a bowl with 2 tablespoons mayonnaise, 1 tablespoon mustard, and 2 tablespoons chopped mixed herbs (as above), then spread over 4 slices of bread. Top with 4 slices of deli ham and cover each with a second piece of bread. Heat gently in a nonstick skillet for 6–7 minutes, turning once, until the bread is golden brown and the inside is hot and melted. Cut in half and serve.

30 Cheese and Onion Broiled Ham

Heat 2 tablespoons oil in a large, nonstick skillet and cook 4 ham steaks (about 6 oz each), for 6–7 minutes, turning once, until cooked and golden. Remove from the skillet and set aside. Add 1 sliced onion to the skillet and cook gently for 10–12 minutes, until soft and golden. Stir in 2 tablespoons chopped mixed herbs, 2 tablespoons whole-grain mustard, and 1 cup low-sodium vegetable stock, then simmer for 2–3 minutes to reduce slightly. Arrange the ham steaks in a shallow ovenproof dish and spoon the onion and herb mixture over the top, pouring over the juices. Top with ²⁄₃ cup shredded cheddar cheese and cook under a preheated broiler for 3–4 minutes, until melted and golden. Serve with crusty bread, tomatoes, and lettuce.

Pan-Fried Gnocchi and Chorizo Salad

Serves 4

2 tablespoons olive oil

1 (16 oz) package gnocchi

4 large, ripe tomatoes, coarsely chopped

1 small bunch of basil leaves, coarsely shredded

4 oz mozzarella cheese, torn into pieces

4 oz sliced chorizo

1–2 tablespoons balsamic vinegar

salt and pepper

- Heat the olive oil in a large, nonstick skillet and add the gnocchi. Sauté for about 8 minutes, moving frequently, until crisp and golden.

- Meanwhile, toss the tomatoes with the basil leaves and torn mozzarella, season with salt and pepper, and arrange on 4 serving plates.

- Add the chorizo to the pan of gnocchi for the final 1–2 minutes of cooking, until slightly crisp and golden. Divide the gnocchi and chorizo among the salads, and serve drizzled with a little balsamic vinegar.

Fried Gnocchi with Chorizo and Tomato Sauce Heat 2 tablespoons oil in a large, nonstick skillet and cook 1 chopped red onion for 7–8 minutes, until soft and golden. Chop 4 oz chorizo, add to the skillet, and cook for 1–2 minutes. Dice 4 large tomatoes, add to the skillet with 1 tablespoon balsamic vinegar, and reduce the heat. Cook gently for 3–4 minutes, then stir in the leaves from a small bunch of basil, season with salt and pepper, and remove from the heat. Meanwhile, sauté 1 (16 oz) package gnocchi in a separate skillet, following the main recipe. Spoon the gnocchi into 4 shallow bowls, spoon the chorizo and tomato sauce over the pasta, and serve sprinkleed with 4 oz mozzarella cheese, torn into pieces.

Creamy Gnocchi and Chorizo Casserole Dice 4 large tomatoes and place in a large bowl with 4 oz sliced chorizo, 1½ (16 oz) packages gnocchi, 1 small bunch of basil leaves, coarsely shredded, and 1–2 tablespoons balsamic vinegar. Season generously, then transfer to a large casserole, pour ½ cup ight cream over the top, and sprinkle with 4 oz mozzarella cheese, torn into pieces. Cook in a preheated oven, at 400°F, for about 20 minutes until bubbling and golden. Serve with plenty of mixed salad greens.

20 Sesame Chicken and Noodles

Serves 4

1 lb skinless, boneless chicken breasts or thighs, cut into thin strips

2 teaspoons cornstarch

1 tablespoon dark soy sauce

1½ tablespoons sesame oil

2 teaspoons sesame seeds, plus extra to serve

2 teaspoons honey

2 tablespoons vegetable oil

1 onion, halved and thinly sliced

1 red bell pepper, cored, seeded, and thinly sliced

2 small zucchini, thinly sliced

1 tablespoon finely chopped fresh ginger root (optional)

1 lb medium dried egg noodles

½ cup water

- Mix the chicken with the cornstarch, soy sauce, 1 tablespoon of the sesame oil, the sesame seeds, and honey. Let marinate.

- Heat the vegetable oil in a skillet or wok and sauté the onion and red bell pepper for 3–4 minutes, until slightly softened. Add the zucchini and ginger, if using, and cook for another 4–5 minutes, stirring frequently, until slightly softened.

- Meanwhile, bring a large saucepan of water to a boil, add the egg noodles, and immediately remove from the heat. Cover and set aside for 4–5 minutes, until tender. Alternatively, cook according to the package directions. Drain and refresh under cold water, then toss in the remaining sesame oil.

- Add the chicken and its marinade to the vegetables and cook gently for 1–2 minutes to seal. Stir in the measured water and simmer gently for 2–3 minutes, until the chicken is cooked through and the sauce thickened.

- Add the noodles to the skillet and cook for 1–2 minutes, until hot, then mound into bowls and serve sprinkled with extra sesame seeds.

 Chicken Noodle Salad Cook and cool 1 lb medium dried egg noodles, following the main recipe. Toss with 1 sliced red bell pepper, 2 sliced scallions, 1½ cups bean sprouts, and 2 cups cooked chicken strips. Mix together 2 tablespoons vegetable oil, 1½ tablespoons sesame oil, 2 teaspoons honey, 1 tablespoon dark soy sauce, and 1 teaspoon finely grated fresh ginger root and toss into the noodle salad. Serve sprinkled with sesame seeds.

Velvet Sesame Chicken Whisk 1 tablespoon cornstarch and 1 egg white until foamy. Stir in 1 lb cubed chicken breast and set aside at room temperature for at least 15 minutes. Drain the chicken on paper towels and pat dry. Heat 2 tablespoons vegetable oil in a large, nonstick skillet and cook the chicken for 3–4 minutes, until golden. Add 1 sliced yellow bell pepper and 1 sliced onion and cook for an additional 3–4 minutes, until beginning to soften. Add 3½ cups small broccoli florets and 1 tablespoon chopped fresh ginger root and cook for 4–5 minutes, stirring frequently, until slightly softened. Stir in 1½ tablespoons sesame oil, 2 teaspoons honey, 1 tablespoon dark soy sauce, and ½ cup water and simmer gently for 2–3 minutes, until the chicken is completely cooked and the sauce thickened slightly. Spoon the chicken over bowls of hot, cooked noodles and sprinkle with sesame seeds to serve.

BUD-MEAT-MUI

30 Ham and Mushroom Risotto

Serves 4

5 cups boiling ham stock or
vegetable stock
½ oz dried porcini mushrooms
or mixed dried mushrooms
(optional)
2 tablespoons olive oil
1 onion, chopped
1 garlic clove, chopped
3 cups chopped mushrooms
1¾ cups risotto rice
½ cup dry white wine
8 oz cooked ham off the bone,
chopped
½ cup mascarpone or
cream cheese
salt and pepper
finely grated Parmesan-style
cheese, to serve (optional)

- Pour the stock into a saucepan, add the dried mushrooms, if using, cover, and simmer gently for 8–10 minutes. If not using the dried mushrooms, pour the stock into the pan and keep at a gentle simmer.

- Heat the oil in a large skillet and add the onion and garlic. Cook for 4–5 minutes, then add the chopped mushrooms and cook for an additional 2–3 minutes, until softened. Add the rice and stir for a minute, until the grains are coated and translucent. Pour in the wine and simmer rapidly, stirring, until the liquid has been absorbed. Meanwhile, strain the dried mushrooms, if using, set aside, and return the stock to the pan.

- Add the hot stock to the rice, a ladleful at a time, stirring continuously at a gentle simmer until each ladleful has been absorbed. Repeat this process until all of the stock has been absorbed and the rice is al dente. This should take 17 minutes.

- Chop the dried mushrooms, if using, and stir into the risotto with the ham and mascarpone and season generously. Stir to warm through, then remove from the heat, cover with a lid, and set aside to rest for 2–3 minutes. Spoon the risotto into bowls and serve with a little grated cheese, if desired.

 Quick Ham and Mushroom Risotto

Heat 1 tablespoon oil in a skillet and cook 1 chopped onion and 1 chopped garlic clove for 4–5 minutes. Add 3 cups chopped mushrooms and cook for an additional 2 minutes. Stir in 5 oz chopped ham, ½ cup mascarpone, 3 cups cooked rice, and 1 cup hot vegetable stock. Stir until heated, season, and serve.

 Ham and Mushroom Fried

Rice Cook 2 cups quick-cooking long-grain rice according to the package directions, until just tender, then drain well. Heat 2 tablespoons vegetable oil in a large, deep skillet, add 1 chopped onion and 1 chopped garlic clove, and cook for 4–5 minutes. Add 3 cups chopped mushrooms and cook for an additional 2–3 minutes, until softened.

Add 2 tablespoons vegetable oil and the rice to the skillet with 1 cup defrosted frozen peas and 8 oz chopped cooked ham. Stir-fry for 3–4 minutes, stirring continuously, until lightly golden. Season with pepper and 2–3 teaspoons light soy sauce and serve in shallow bowls.

30 Simple Sausage, Bean, and Vegetable Stew

Serves 4

2 tablespoons vegetable oil

1 red onion, halved and sliced

2 garlic cloves, sliced

6 Italian-style link sausages

1 large red bell pepper, cored, seeded, and cut into quarters

1 (14½ oz) can diced tomatoes

1 (15 oz) can chickpeas or lima beans, drained and rinsed

2 teaspoons chopped rosemary or 1 teaspoon dried rosemary

1 ham, vegetable, or beef bouillon cube

1 cup hot water

steamed green vegetables, to serve (optional)

- Heat the oil in a deep skillet and cook the onion for 4 minutes. Add the garlic and cook for an additional 1–2 minutes, until slightly softened.

- Meanwhile, arrange the sausages on a foil-lined broiler rack with the red bell pepper pieces and cook under a preheated broiler for 5–6 minutes, turning regularly, until browned. Cool slightly, then thickly slice the sausages diagonally and coarsely chop the bell peppers.

- Pour the diced tomatoes into the skillet with the onions, then add the chickpeas or lima beans, rosemary, bouillon cube, measured water, sausages, and bell peppers. Cover with a lid, bring to a boil, then reduce the heat and simmer gently for 15–20 minutes, until thickened.

- Spoon the sausage and vegetable stew into 4 shallow bowls and serve with a selection of steamed green vegetables, if desired.

 Warm Chorizo and Bean Stew Heat 2 tablespoons oil in a skillet, add 1 sliced red onion, and cook for 4 minutes. Add 4 oz diced chorizo and 2 sliced garlic cloves and cook for an additional 1–2 minutes. Meanwhile, quarter 1 red bell pepper and cook under a preheated broiler for 5–6 minutes, turning. Mix 1 (15 oz) can chickpeas with 3 diced tomatoes and 2 tablespoons chopped parsley. Season, then add to the skillet and cook for 1–2 minutes. Spoon into 4 shallow dishes, top with the roasted peppers, and serve.

Broiled Sausages with Bean Stew Arrange 8 spicy sausages on a foil-lined broiler rack and cook under a preheated broiler for 16–18 minutes, turning occasionally, until cooked through, adding 1 red bell pepper, cut into quarters, for the final 5–6 minutes. Meanwhile, heat 2 tablespoons oil in a large, nonstick skillet and cook 1 sliced red onion and 2 sliced garlic cloves for 4–5 minutes, until softened and lightly golden. Add 1 (14½ oz) can diced tomatoes, 1 (15 oz) can chickpeas or lima beans, drained and rinsed, 2 teaspoons chopped rosemary, 1 bouillon cube, and 1 cup hot water to the skillet, then bring to a boil, reduce the heat, and simmer gently for about 12–15 minutes, until thickened slightly. Spoon into bowls and serve with the broiled sausages and peppers.

30 Baked Eggplant with Lamb and Pine Nuts

Serves 4

⅓ cup olive oil or vegetable oil
2 eggplants (about 12 oz each),
   halved lengthwise
1 onion, chopped
2 garlic cloves, sliced
3 tablespoons pine nuts
1 lb ground lamb
2 teaspoons ground cumin
½ teaspoon ground cinnamon
3 tablespoons chopped mint
3 tablespoons dry white wine
⅔ cup crumbled feta cheese
salt and pepper

To serve

steamed couscous
lemon wedges

- Preheat the oven to 400°F. Heat 3 tablespoons of the oil in a large skillet and cook the eggplants, cut sides down, for 5 minutes, until golden, then turn and cook the other sides for 2–3 minutes. Transfer them, cut sides up, to an ovenproof dish and season generously. Cook in the preheated oven for 8–10 minutes.

- Meanwhile, wipe the skillet clean and heat the remaining oil in it. Add the onion and garlic and cook for 5–6 minutes. Add the pine nuts and cook for 1–2 minutes, until golden.

- Add the ground lamb to the skillet with the ground cumin and cinnamon and sauté over medium-high heat, stirring frequently, for 5–6 minutes, until browned. Stir in the chopped mint and season lightly.

- Remove the eggplants from the oven, spoon the lamb mixture over the top, and pour the white wine over them. Sprinkle with the feta and return to the oven for an additional 10–15 minutes, until bubbling and lightly golden. Serve with lemon wedges and steamed couscous.

 Grilled Lamb with Pine Nuts

Mix ⅓ cup olive oil with 2 teaspoons ground cumin, ½ teaspoon ground cinnamon, grated rind of 1 lemon, and salt and pepper, and rub into 4 lamb cutlets. Heat a ridged grill pan and cook the lamb for 3–4 minutes on each side. Sprinkle with 3 tablespoons pine nuts, 3 tablespoons chopped mint, and ⅔ cup crumbled feta cheese, and serve with couscous and lemon wedges.

 Lamb, Eggplant, and Pine Nut Burgers Place 1 lb ground lamb in a bowl with 1 cup fresh bread crumbs, 1 finely chopped onion, 1 crushed garlic clove, 1 tablespoon pine nuts, 1 beaten egg, 2 teaspoons ground cumin, ½ teaspoon ground cinnamon, 3 tablespoons chopped mint, and seasoning. Mix well and form into 4 patties. Heat 1 tablespoon oil in a nonstick skillet and cook the patties for 4–5 minutes each side, until browned and cooked through. Meanwhile, cut 1 eggplant into ¼-inch slices and cook on a preheated ridged grill pan for 7–8 minutes, turning occasionally, until charred and softened. Remove from the heat, drizzle with 1 tablespoon oil, and season with salt and pepper. Grill the cut sides of 4 halved burger buns, and serve the burgers in the buns in between slices of eggplant and 4 oz sliced feta cheese.

QuickCook
Fish and Seafood

Recipes listed by cooking time

30

20

10

3⓪ Tuna Cakes with Cilantro Mayonnaise

Serves 4

4–5 scallions, chopped
1 garlic clove, coarsely chopped
¾-inch piece fresh ginger root,
    peeled and chopped
1 red chile, seeded and chopped
3 tablespoons vegetable oil
1 (12 oz) can tuna, drained
⅓ cup cooked white rice
1 cup fresh bread crumbs
2 tablespoons sweet chili sauce
1 egg, lightly beaten
1 tablespoon chopped cilantro
2–3 tablespoons all-purpose flour
handful of arugula, to garnish

For the cilantro mayonnaise

3 tablespoons mayonnaise
1 tablespoon chopped cilantro
2 teaspoons lime juice
    or lemon juice
salt and pepper

- Place the scallions in a mini chopper or the small bowl of a food processor with the garlic, ginger, and chile, and pulse briefly, until finely chopped. Alternatively, chop finely by hand. Heat 1 tablespoon of the oil in a small skillet and cook the mixture for 2–3 minutes, until aromatic and slightly softened. Set aside to cool slightly.

- Meanwhile, place the tuna in a large bowl with the rice, bread crumbs, chili sauce, egg, and cilantro. Add the cooked onion mixture and mix gently to combine. Shape into 12 oblong cakes, cover, and chill in the refrigerator for about 12 minutes.

- To make the cilantro mayonnaise, spoon the mayonnaise into a small bowl and stir in the cilantro and the lime juice or lemon juice. Season with salt and pepper and set aside.

- Heat the remaining oil in a large nonstick skillet. Dust the tuna cakes lightly in the flour and cook for 6–7 minutes, turning occasionally, until crisp and golden. Serve the cakes hot with the cilantro mayonnaise and garnish with arugula.

1⓪ Zesty Tuna Rice Salad Peel and grate a ¾-inch piece of fresh ginger root, crush 1 small garlic clove, and seed and finely chop 1 red chile, then place in a bowl with 3 tablespoons vegetable oil and 2 tablespoons lime juice. Whisk to combine. In a large bowl, mix 3 cups cooked rice with 4–5 finely sliced scallions, 1 finely chopped red bell pepper, and 1 (12 oz) can tuna, drained and flaked. Fold in the dressing and serve immediately.

2⓪ Spicy Fresh Tuna Burgers Place 10 oz tuna fillet in a food processor with 1 teaspoon Thai red curry paste and 2 tablespoons chopped fresh cilantro and pulse briefly, until finely chopped. Transfer to a bowl and mix gently with 1 small beaten egg, 2 finely chopped scallions, ⅓ cup cooked white rice, and 1 cup fresh bread crumbs, then form into 4 patties. Heat 3 tablespoons vegetable oil in a large nonstick skillet and cook the patties for 2–3 minutes each side, until just cooked and golden. Serve in toasted buns with the cilantro mayonnaise from the main recipe and some salad greens.

10 Shrimp, Avocado, and Cilantro Tostada

Serves 4

4 large soft flour tortillas
1 small iceberg lettuce, shredded
10 oz cooked, peeled shrimp
1 large, ripe but firm avocado, peeled and diced
2 tablespoons chopped fresh cilantro
1 tablespoon lime juice
salt and cracked black pepper
lime wedges, to serve

- Heat a ridged grill pan and toast a tortilla for 30–60 seconds on each side, until lightly charred. Immediately push it into a small, deep bowl and set aside. Repeat with the remaining tortillas to make 4 bowl-shaped tortillas. Place one-quarter of the shredded lettuce inside each one.

- Meanwhile, toss together the shrimp, avocado, cilantro, and lime juice and season with salt and pepper. Divide among the tortillas and serve with the lime wedges.

20 Shrimp and Black Bean Chili

Heat 2 tablespoons vegetable oil in a large skillet and add 4 chopped scallions, 2 chopped garlic cloves, and 1 finely chopped and seeded red chile. Cook gently for 2 minutes, until softened, then add 1 (14½ oz) can diced tomatoes and 1 (15 oz) can black beans, drained and rinsed. Simmer gently for 10–12 minutes, until thickened slightly. Stir in 3 tablespoons chopped cilantro, 1 tablespoon lime juice, and 8 oz cooked, peeled shrimp. Simmer for 1 minute, until the shrimp are hot, and serve with grilled tortillas and lime wedges, sprinkled with extra cilantro.

30 Mexican Shrimp Rice with Avocado

Salad Heat 2 tablespoons vegetable oil in a large saucepan or casserole and gently cook 4 chopped scallions, 2 chopped garlic cloves, and 1 finely chopped and seeded red chile for 2 minutes. Stir 1⅓ cups long-grain rice and 1 (1¼ oz) envelope mild fajita spice mix into the pan, then add 1 (14½ oz) can diced tomatoes and 2½ cups hot vegetable stock. Stir to combine, then bring to a boil, reduce the heat, and cover with a tight-fitting lid. Simmer gently for 20–25 minutes, until the rice is tender, adding 8 oz cooked, peeled shrimp for the last minute. Meanwhile, toss 1 peeled and diced avocado gently with 1 tablespoon lime juice and 2 tablespoons chopped fresh cilantro. Serve the rice in bowls topped with a spoonful of avocado salad and grilled tortillas.

 # Smoked Mackerel Brandade

Serves 4

6 medium floury potatoes
   (about 1½ lb), such as russets,
   peeled and cut into chunks
2–3 cups hot milk
2 garlic cloves, sliced
5 oz smoked mackerel fillets,
   skin removed
⅔ cup crème fraîche
3 tablespoons chopped parsley
¼ cup olive oil
salt and pepper
hot toast, to serve

- Place the potatoes in medium saucepan and pour enough milk over them to cover. Add the sliced garlic and a little seasoning, then bring to a boil and cook for about 15 minutes, or until tender.

- Meanwhile, place the smoked mackerel in the small bowl of a food processor with the crème fraîche and blend until smooth. Stir in the chopped parsley and plenty of cracked black pepper.

- Drain the potatoes, reserving the milk. Return the potatoes to the pan with ¼ cup of the milk and the olive oil, and mash until smooth. Mix in the mackerel and season with salt and pepper. Spoon into 4 small bowls and serve immediately with plenty of hot toast.

Smoked Mackerel Pâté Place 5 oz smoked mackerel in a food processor with ⅔ cup cream cheese, 1 tablespoon creamed horseradish, 2 teaspoons lemon juice, and 3 tablespoons chopped parsley. Blend until almost smooth, then season with salt and pepper. Serve the pâté accompanied by plenty of hot toast.

Hot Mackerel Brandade Casserole Place 6 medium floury potatoes (about 1½ lb), such as russets, peeled and cut into chunks, in a medium saucepan and pour enough milk over them to cover. Add 2 sliced garlic cloves and season with salt and pepper, then bring to a boil and cook for about 10 minutes, until just tender but still firm. Drain and put into a casserole. Sprinkle with 5 oz flaked smoked mackerel fillets. Mix 3 tablespoons chopped parsley with 1¾ cups crème fraîche, season with salt and pepper, and pour over the potatoes. Sprinkle with 1¼ cups shredded Swiss cheese or cheddar cheese and cook in a preheated oven, at 400°F, for 15–20 minutes, until bubbling and golden. Serve with a salad.

30 Easy Fish Casserole with Crunchy Potato Topping

Serves 4

6 medium potatoes (about 1½ lb), unpeeled

8 oz white fish fillet, such as cod, pollock, or red snapper, cut into bite-size pieces

8 oz salmon fillet, cut into bite-size pieces

1¾ cups hot milk

4 tablespoons butter

⅓ cup plus 1 tablespoon flour

1 cup shredded cheddar cheese

2 teaspoons lemon juice

2 tablespoons chopped chives

4 oz small cooked, peeled shrimp (optional)

salt and pepper

- Preheat the oven to 350°F. Cook the potatoes in a large saucepan of lightly salted water for 6–7 minutes. Drain and set aside to cool slightly.

- Meanwhile, place the fish in a deep skillet. Pour over the hot milk and bring to a boil. Reduce the heat and simmer gently for 3–4 minutes, until the fish is just cooked. Strain the milk into a large measuring cup and transfer the fish to a casserole.

- Place the butter and flour in a saucepan and warm gently to melt the butter. Stir over the heat to cook the flour for 2 minutes, then add the milk a little at a time, stirring well to incorporate. Stir over the heat for 2–3 minutes, until thickened, then remove from the heat and stir in half the cheese, the lemon juice, and chives, and season with salt and pepper. Pour the sauce over the fish, add the shrimp, if using, and stir gently to coat.

- Wearing rubber gloves to protect your hands from the heat, grate the potatoes coarsely and sprinkle over the fish. Sprinkle with the remaining cheese and cook in the preheated oven for 15–20 minutes, until the topping is golden and crispy.

1 Easy Fried Fish
Heat 2 tablespoons oil in a large nonstick skillet and cook 4 chunky salmon or white fish fillets (about 5 oz each), for about 3 minutes on each side, until just cooked. Season generously. Serve on warm plates with 1 (24 oz) store-bought mashed potatoes and drizzled with 1½ cups store-bought cheese sauce.

2 Easy Baked Fish
Place 4 chunky salmon or white fish fillets (about 5 oz each), on a greased baking sheet. In a bowl, mix together 1 cup fresh bread crumbs with the grated rind of 1 lemon, 2 tablespoons chopped chives, 1 tablespoon olive oil, and some seasoning. Pile the bread crumb mixture on top of the fish fillets and cook in a preheated oven, at 400°F, for 12–15 minutes, until the fish is cooked and the topping golden. Meanwhile, cook 8 medium potatoes (about 2 lb), peeled and cut into small chunks, in a large saucepan of lightly salted boiling water for about 15 minutes, until tender. Mash until smooth with 4 tablespoons butter, 1 tablespoon lemon juice, and 3 tablespoons heavy cream or milk. Season with salt and pepper and serve topped with the crunchy fish fillets.

Tomato, Mussel, and Eggplant Shells

Serves 4

¼ cup olive oil or vegetable oil
2 garlic cloves, chopped
1 large onion, finely chopped
1 red chile, seeded and finely chopped
1 (14½ oz) can diced tomatoes
½ cup water
1 teaspoon finely grated lemon rind
pinch of sugar
1 lb pasta shells
1 eggplant, diced
8 oz cooked shelled mussels

- Heat half the oil in a saucepan, add the chopped garlic, onion, and chile, and cook for 1–2 minutes, until just softened. Add the tomatoes, measured water, lemon rind, and sugar, then season to taste and simmer gently for 15–18 minutes.

- Cook the pasta shells in a large saucepan of lightly salted boiling water according to package directions, until al dente.

- Meanwhile, heat the remaining oil in a large skillet and cook the eggplant for about 8 minutes, turning occasionally, until golden. Transfer to the simmering pan of tomato sauce for the remaining cooking time.

- Stir the mussels into the tomato sauce for the final minute, cook until thoroughly heated through, then spoon over the drained pasta to serve.

 Tomato and Mussel Fusilli

Cook 1 lb quick-cooking fusilli pasta according to package directions. Heat ¼ cup olive oil or vegetable oil in a saucepan, add 2 chopped garlic cloves and 1 seeded and finely chopped red chile, and cook for 1–2 minutes. Add 10 oz defrosted frozen mussels, cook for 1 minute, then stir in 4 diced tomatoes, 1 teaspoon finely grated lemon rind, and 1 tablespoon lemon juice. Season generously to taste, then toss immediately with the drained pasta and spoon into bowls to serve.

 Cheesy Baked Mussel and Eggplant Pasta Make the mussel and eggplant sauce following the main recipe. Cook 1 lb fusilli or penne pasta according to package directions, until al dente, then drain. Toss with the pasta sauce and transfer to a large ovenproof dish. Arrange 8 oz thinly sliced mozzarella over the top and drizzle with 1 tablespoon oil. Cook under a preheated broiler for 6–7 minutes, until lightly golden and melted. Serve with an arugula salad.

BUD-FISH-TAQ

Skillet Pizza with Anchovies

Serves 4

2⅓ cups all-purpose flour,
  plus extra for dusting
1 tablespoon baking powder
1 teaspoon dried thyme
⅔ cup warm water
1½ tablespoons olive oil
⅓ cup store-bought pizza sauce
  or tomato pasta sauce
1 (2 oz) can anchovies, drained
2 tablespoons capers, drained
  and rinsed
1 cup diced mozzarella cheese
salt and pepper

- Mix the flour and baking powder in a bowl with the thyme and a generous pinch of salt and pepper. Pour in the warm water and olive oil, and mix to form a soft dough.

- Divide the dough in half and roll out on a lightly floured surface to fit 2 large nonstick skillets, approximately 11 inches across. Dust with a little flour. Heat the skillets over medium heat and lower the circles of dough carefully into the skillets. Cook for about 10 minutes, turning once, until lightly golden.

- Spread the sauce over the pizza crusts and sprinkle with the anchovies and capers. Sprinkle with the mozzarella and cook under a preheated broiler for 3–5 minutes, until golden and bubbling. Serve immediately.

Anchovy and Black Olive Tapenade

Place 1 cup pitted black olives in a mini chopper or the small bowl of a food processor with 6 drained anchovy fillets, 2 tablespoons drained and rinsed capers, 1 crushed garlic clove, and ½ teaspoon dried thyme. Blend to a smooth paste and stir in 2 tablespoons oil and 1 teaspoon lemon juice. Spread the tapenade over slices of French bread and serve topped with mozzarella.

Mini Tuna and Anchovy Pizzas

Make the dough following the main recipe, then divide into approximately 16 small balls. Roll out each ball thinly and arrange on 2 lightly floured baking sheets. Cook in a preheated oven, at 400°F, for 3–4 minutes, until lightly golden. Spread ⅓ cup store-bought pizza sauce or tomato pasta sauce on the mini pizzas, then drain 1 (5 oz) can tuna and divide between them. Top each one with 1 chopped anchovy fillet and a little mozzarella, then return to the oven for 8–10 minutes, until the pizzas are crisp and melting. Serve hot with a leafy green salad.

BUD-FISH-GOK

 # Teriyaki Salmon Sticks with Bean Sprout Salad

Serves 4

1 lb skinless, boneless salmon fillet, cut into bite-size pieces

½ cup teriyaki marinade

1 tablespoon sesame oil or vegetable oil, plus extra for greasing

2 cups bean sprouts

2 carrots, peeled and shredded

2 scallions, chopped

3 tablespoons coarsely chopped cilantro

1 tablespoon rice wine vinegar or white wine vinegar

- Place the salmon in a bowl with three-quarters of the teriyaki marinade. Mix to coat and set aside for 10 minutes. Lightly grease a baking sheet.

- Meanwhile, mix the bean sprouts, carrots, scallions, and cilantro in a large bowl. Combine the remaining teriyaki marinade with the vegetable oil and vinegar in a small bowl to make a dressing.

- Thread the salmon pieces onto 4 metal skewers and arrange on the greased baking sheet. Cook under a preheated broiler for about 8 minutes, turning occasionally, until almost cooked through.

- Toss the salad with the dressing and arrange on 4 plates, then serve with the hot salmon skewers.

 ### Smoked Salmon and Teriyaki Salad

Mix 2 cups bean sprouts, 2 coarsely grated carrots, 2 chopped scallions, and 3 tablespoons chopped cilantro in a large bowl. Combine 2 tablespoons teriyaki marinade with 1 tablespoon sesame oil and 1 tablespoon rice wine vinegar to make a dressing. Slice 8 oz smoked salmon into strips. Divide the salad among 4 plates, sprinkle the smoked salmon over the salad, and drizzle with the dressing.

 ### Teriyaki Salmon Packages

Cut 1 lb skinless, boneless salmon fillet into 4 pieces and place in a shallow dish. Combine ½ cup teriyaki marinade with 1 tablespoon sesame oil and 1 tablespoon rice wine vinegar, pour over the salmon, mix to coat, and set aside for 10 minutes. Meanwhile, cut 2 carrots and 2 scallions into thin matchsticks and thinly shred half a Chinese cabbage. Toss the vegetables in a large bowl with 2 cups bean sprouts and 3 tablespoons coarsely chopped cilantro, then divide among 4 large squares of foil. Top each pile of vegetables with a salmon fillet, then drizzle with any leftover marinade. Fold up the sides of the foil and scrunch together to make 4 packages. Place on a baking sheet and cook in a preheated oven, at 400°F, for 12–15 minutes, until the salmon is just cooked through and the vegetables have softened. Serve with a bowl of steamed rice, if desired.

BUD-FISH-JUO

Thai-Flavored Mussels with Coconut Milk

Serves 4

2 tablespoons vegetable oil

2 shallots, halved and finely sliced

1-inch piece of fresh ginger root, peeled and finely chopped

1 garlic clove, finely sliced

1 green chile, seeded and finely sliced

1 cup coconut milk

2 teaspoons Thai fish sauce

1¼ cups vegetable stock

2 lb mussels, scrubbed, and any unopened shells discarded

1 small bunch of cilantro, coarsely chopped, to garnish (optional)

- Heat the oil in a large saucepan or casserole and cook the shallots, ginger, garlic, and chile gently for 6–8 minutes, until really soft.

- Add the coconut milk, fish sauce, and stock and heat to boiling point. Simmer gently for 5–6 minutes to let the flavors develop, then stir in the mussels. Cover with a tight-fitting lid and let cook gently for 4–5 minutes, shaking the pan occasionally, until all the mussels have opened, discarding any that remain closed.

- Spoon into large, shallow bowls with the coconut-flavored soup and serve immediately sprinkled with cilantro, if using.

Thai Green Curry Mussels Heat 2 tablespoons vegetable oil in a large casserole or saucepan and add 2 tablespoons Thai green curry paste. Pour in 1 cup coconut milk and 1¼ cups hot vegetable stock, bring to a boil, and add 2 lb scrubbed mussels. Cover and cook gently for 4–5 minutes, shaking the pan occasionally, until all the mussels have opened. Serve immediately, sprinkled with chopped cilantro, if desired.

Thai-Flavored Mussel and Noodle Soup In a large saucepan, heat 4 cups vegetable stock or chicken stock with 3 tablespoons Thai fish sauce, 1 tablespoon light brown sugar, the finely chopped stems from a bunch of cilantro, 2 finely sliced shallots, 1 finely sliced garlic clove, a peeled and finely chopped 1-inch piece of fresh ginger root, and 1 seeded and finely sliced green chile. Simmer gently for about 20 minutes to let the flavors develop. Meanwhile, cook 10 oz rice noodles according to the package directions, and divide among 4 deep, warm bowls. Strain the soup through a strainer and return to the pan with 1 cup coconut milk and 7 oz cooked shelled mussels. Heat for 1–2 minutes, until the mussels are hot, then stir in 2 tablespoons lime juice and ladle over the bowls of noodles. Serve immediately, sprinkled with the chopped cilantro leaves.

 # Chile and Anchovy Dressed Pasta

Serves 4

1 lb quick-cook spaghetti
3 tablespoons olive oil
2 garlic cloves, chopped
1 red chile, seeded and
 finely sliced
2 tablespoons lemon juice
3 tablespoons chopped flat
 leaf parsley
1 (2 oz) can anchovy fillets in oil,
 drained and coarsely chopped
pepper

- Cook the spaghetti in a large saucepan of lightly salted boiling water according to package directions, until al dente.

- Meanwhile, heat the olive oil in a small saucepan and add the garlic and chile. Simmer gently in the oil for 2 minutes, until softened, then remove from the heat.

- Drain the pasta and toss immediately with the garlic and chile oil, lemon juice, parsley, and chopped anchovies. Season with pepper and serve in warm bowls.

 Chile and Anchovy Grilled Fish

Place 4 chunky, skinless, boneless white fish fillets on a board and top each with 2 anchovy fillets. Sprinkle with 3 tablespoons chopped parsley, 1 seeded, sliced red chile, and the finely grated rind of 1 lemon. Wrap each fillet in a large slice of prosciutto and drizzle with 1 tablespoon olive oil. Heat a ridged grill pan and cook the packages for 7–8 minutes, turning occasionally, until just cooked through. Meanwhile, cook 1 lb quick-cook spaghetti according to the package directions. Drain and toss in 2 tablespoons olive oil and 2 tablespoons lemon juice. Season with salt and pepper. Mound into 4 warm bowls and top each with a grilled cod and anchovy package.

 Chile, Anchovy, and Roasted Red Pepper Pasta Cut 3 red bell peppers in half and arrange them, cut side up, in a large roasting pan. Fill each bell pepper half with 2 cherry tomatoes, a little chopped garlic, 1 anchovy fillet, and a sprinkleing of chopped red chile. Drizzle with 3 tablespoons olive oil and 2 tablespoons lemon juice and cook in a preheated oven, at 400°F, for 20 minutes, until slightly softened. Meanwhile, cook 1 lb spaghetti in a large saucepan of lightly salted boiling water according to package directions, until al dente. Transfer the filled roasted peppers to a food processor, pulse briefly to make a coarsely chopped sauce, and toss quickly with the drained pasta. Mound into bowls and serve immediately, sprinkled with chopped parsley.

30 Salmon Fish Cakes with Tartare Sauce

Serves 4

3 medium potatoes, peeled and cut into chunks

2 (6 oz) cans salmon, drained

2 tablespoons chopped mixed herbs, such as chives, tarragon, and parsley

3 tablespoons minced pickles

1 tablespoon capers, rinsed and finely chopped

⅓ cup all-purpose flour

1 extra-large egg, lightly beaten

1⅓ cups fresh bread crumbs

oil, for pan-frying

salt and pepper

handful of arugula, to garnish

For the tartare sauce

⅓ cup mayonnaise

1 tablespoon lemon juice

1 tablespoon capers, rinsed and finely chopped

3 tablespoons chopped pickles

- Cook the potatoes in a large saucepan of lightly salted boiling water for about 12 minutes, until tender. Drain well, mash until almost smooth, then let cool slightly.

- Meanwhile, flake the salmon into a bowl and add the herbs, pickles, and capers. Season generously with salt and pepper, then mix gently with the potatoes and form into 8 fish cakes. Dust in the flour, dip both sides in the beaten egg to coat, then turn in the bread crumbs to cover. Cover loosely with plastic wrap and chill for about 10 minutes.

- Meanwhile, make the tartare sauce by combining together all the ingredients in a bowl. Season with salt and pepper and set aside.

- Heat the oil in a large nonstick skillet and cook the fish cakes for 2–3 minutes each side, until crisp and golden. Garnish with arugula and serve with the tartare sauce.

 Smoked Salmon Rillettes Place 8 oz smoked salmon pieces in a food processor with 2 tablespoons chopped fresh herbs, 2 teaspoons lemon juice, 1 tablespoon chopped pickles, and 1 teaspoon drained and rinsed capers and pulse until finely chopped. Add ⅔ cup cream cheese and some black pepper and blend until almost smooth. Scrape into 4 small ramekins and serve with crispbreads.

 Baked Salmon with Capers Mix 2 tablespoons chopped fresh mixed herbs in a small bowl with 1 tablespoon capers, 1 tablespoon finely chopped pickles, and ½ cup cream cheese. Place 4 chunky salmon fillets (about 5 oz each) in an ovenproof dish and cut a deep slit down the middle of each one to make a pocket, then stuff with the cream cheese mixture. Season and cook in a preheated oven, at 400°F, for 12–15 minutes, until the salmon is cooked through. Meanwhile, cook 8 medium potatoes (about 2 lb), peeled, in a saucepan of lightly salted boiling water for 12–15 minutes, until tender. Drain and mash until smooth with 4 tablespoons butter and ¼ cup light cream. Spoon the mashed potatoes onto 4 plates, top with the cooked salmon fillets, and squeeze a little lemon juice over the fish. Serve immediately with prepared tartare sauce.

BUD-FISH-FUM

30 Fried Fish with Homemade French Fries and Peas

Serves 4

4 large potatoes (about 2 lb),
   peeled and cut into thick sticks
3 tablespoons vegetable oil
2 tablespoons butter
2 shallots, chopped
2 cups frozen peas
3 tablespoons chopped mixed
   herbs, such as parsley,
   mint, and chives
¼ cup hot vegetable stock
olive oil, for pan-frying
4 pollock, cod, or flounder fillets
   (about 4 oz each)
salt and pepper

- Preheat the oven to 400°F. Cook the prepared potatoes in a large saucepan of lightly salted boiling water for 3 minutes. Drain well and pat dry with a dry dish towel. Toss the potatoes in a large bowl with the vegetable oil and a little salt and pepper. Transfer to a large baking sheet and cook in the preheated oven for 20–25 minutes, turning occasionally, until tender and golden.

- Meanwhile, heat the butter in medium saucepan and cook the shallots for 6–7 minutes, until softened. Add the peas, chopped herbs, and vegetable stock, and season with salt and pepper. Cover and simmer gently for 3–4 minutes, until the peas are tender, then remove from the heat and keep warm.

- Heat the olive oil in a nonstick skillet. Season the fish fillets with a little salt and pepper, then cook gently for about 3 minutes on each side, until golden and only just cooked through. Serve the fish with the French fries and peas.

 Fried Fish with Herbed Pea Puree Cook 3½ cups frozen peas in a saucepan of boiling water for 2–3 minutes, until tender. Drain and put into a food processor with 4 tablespoons butter and 3 tablespoons chopped fresh herbs. Blend until smooth, then put back into the pan and keep warm. Meanwhile, season 4 cod, pollock, or flounder fillets and pan-fry in a little olive oil for about 3 minutes on each side, until golden. Spoon the pea puree onto 4 warm plates and serve with the fish and lemon wedges.

 Baked Fish with Peas Arrange 1½ lb frozen oven fries on a large baking sheet and cook in a preheated oven, at 425°F, for 15–20 minutes, or according to the package directions, until tender and golden. Meanwhile, place 4 pollock, cod, or flounder fillets, skin side down, on a lightly greased baking sheet, drizzle with olive oil, and season with salt and pepper. Bake in the oven for about 10 minutes, until just cooked. While the fries and fish are in the oven, heat 2 tablespoons butter in a medium saucepan and cook 2 chopped shallots for 6–7 minutes, until softened. Add 2 cups frozen peas, 3 tablespoons chopped fresh mixed herbs, and ¼ cup hot vegetable stock. Cover and simmer gently for 3–4 minutes, then drain off the liquid and put the peas into a food processor. Blend until just mushy, then return to the pan, season to taste, and keep warm. Serve the baked fish on warm plates with the peas and oven fries.

Blackened Sardines with Yogurt Dressing

Serves 4

12–16 fresh sardines,
    gutted and scaled
2 teaspoons paprika
1 teaspoon dried oregano
½ teaspoon ground cayenne
    pepper
½ teaspoon dried garlic powder
2 tablespoons olive oil or
    vegetable oil
⅔ cup plain yogurt
2 tablespoons chopped chives
2 tablespoons lime juice
    or lemon juice
salt and pepper

- Use a sharp knife to make 3 slashes in each side of each sardine. Mix together the paprika, oregano, cayenne pepper, garlic powder, and oil, season with salt and pepper, and rub all over the sardines. Set aside to marinate for 8–10 minutes.

- Meanwhile, mix the yogurt with the chives and lime juice or lemon juice, and season with salt and pepper. Set aside.

- Arrange the sardines on a broiler rack and cook under a preheated broiler for 5–6 minutes, turning once, until slightly blackened and cooked through. Serve with the yogurt dressing.

 Sardine and Rice Salad with Yogurt Dressing Drain and flake 4 (3¾ oz) cans sardines and toss with 3 cups cold, cooked rice, 1 finely chopped red bell pepper, and the diced flesh of 1 avocado. Combine ⅔ cup plain yogurt with 2 tablespoons chopped chives and 2 tablespoons lime juice or lemon juice and season to taste. Drizzle the yogurt dressing over the salad before serving.

 Cajun Sardines with Rice Heat 2 tablespoons olive oil or vegetable oil in a large nonstick skillet and add 1 chopped red bell pepper, 1 chopped red onion, and 2 chopped garlic cloves. Cook for 8–9 minutes, or until soft and golden. Add 1 teaspoon dried oregano, ½ teaspoon ground cayenne pepper, and ½ teaspoon dried garlic powder and cook for 1 minute before adding 1 (14½ oz) can diced tomatoes, 3 chopped anchovy fillets in oil, and 1 cup water. Season and simmer gently for about 15 minutes, until thickened. Meanwhile, cook 1⅓ cups long-grain rice in a large saucepan of lightly salted boiling water for about 12 minutes, or according to the package directions, until just tender. Stir 4 (3¾ oz) canned sardines, drained and flaked, into the tomato sauce, heat for 1 minute, and serve spooned over the cooked rice.

Creamy Mustard and Trout Pasta Salad

Serves 4

1 tablespoon light olive oil
4 skinless, boneless trout fillets
(about 4 oz each), lightly
seasoned
1 lb pasta shells
12 cherry tomatoes, halved
½ cucumber, diced

For the dressing

¼ cup mayonnaise
2 tablespoons lemon juice
3 anchovy fillets in oil, drained
and coarsely chopped
1 small garlic clove
1 teaspoon sugar
3 tablespoons grated Parmesan-
style cheese
1 tablespoon whole-grain mustard
½ cup light olive oil or peanut oil
salt and pepper

- Heat the oil in a nonstick skillet and pan-fry the trout fillets for 4–5 minutes, turning once, until just cooked through but still slightly pink in the middle. Remove from the skillet and set aside to cool a little.

- Cook the pasta in a large saucepan of lightly salted boiling water according to the package directions, until al dente. Drain well, refresh under cold running water, and drain again.

- Meanwhile, place the dressing ingredients, except the mustard and oil, in a small food processor and blend until smooth. Transfer to a bowl and slowly whisk in the mustard and oil. Season with salt and pepper.

- Flake the trout into large pieces and toss with the pasta, cherry tomatoes, and cucumber. Spoon into bowls, then drizzle with the mustard dressing and serve immediately.

 Trout and Pasta Caesar Salad

Cook 1 lb quick-cook penne pasta according to the package directions, cool under running water, then drain well and put into a large bowl. Flake 8 oz cooked trout or salmon fillets into the pasta and add ½ diced cucumber, 12 halved cherry tomatoes, and ½ cup prepared Caesar dressing. Mix, then spoon into 4 bowls and serve sprinkled with store-bought croutons, if desired.

 Phyllo-Topped Creamy Mustard Trout Fillets Place 4 chunky trout fillets in a snug-fitting ovenproof dish. Mix 1 tablespoon whole-grain mustard with ⅔ cup cream cheese and spread in a thick layer over the fish. Drizzle with ⅔ cup heavy cream and 1 tablespoon lemon juice. Brush 4 phyllo pastry sheets, about 9 x 10 inches, with 2 tablespoons melted butter and scrunch up the pastry slightly before placing one sheet on top of each fillet.

Cook in a preheated oven, at 350°F, for 18–20 minutes, until the fish is just cooked and the pastry crisp and golden. Make the dressing following the main recipe. Serve the fish on a bed of tagliatelle pasta, drizzled with the creamy mustard sauce.

BUD-FISH-NOF

30 Chile Crab and Rice Cakes with Lime Dipping Sauce

Serves 4

2 (6 oz) cans crabmeat
3 scallions, chopped
¾ cup cooked rice
¾ cup dried bread crumbs
1 red chile, seeded and chopped
3 tablespoons chopped cilantro
finely grated rind of ½ lime
2 medium eggs, lightly beaten
1 teaspoon Thai fish sauce
vegetable oil, for pan-frying
lime wedges, to serve

For the dipping sauce

¼ cup sugar
2 tablespoons rice wine vinegar
   or white wine vinegar
2 tablespoons water
finely grated rind of ½ lime
1 tablespoon lime juice
2 teaspoons Thai fish sauce
½ red chile, seeded and chopped

- In a large bowl, mix the crabmeat, scallions, rice, bread crumbs, chile, cilantro, and half of the lime rind. Add the beaten egg and fish sauce to the bowl and mix to combine, adding extra bread crumbs if the mixture seems a little damp.

- Form the mixture into 12 crab cakes, then arrange on a plate, cover lightly, and chill in the refrigerator for 10–12 minutes, until firm.

- Meanwhile, make the dipping sauce. Place the sugar, vinegar, and measured water in a small saucepan and warm over low heat until the sugar dissolves. Stir in the lime rind and juice, fish sauce, and chile, then remove from the heat and set aside.

- Heat the vegetable oil in a large nonstick skillet and cook the crab cakes for 2–3 minutes on each side, until hot and golden. Drain on paper towels and serve with lime wedges and the dipping sauce.

 Crab and Rice Salad with Lime Dressing

Flake 2 (6 oz) cans crabmeat, and toss with 3 chopped scallions, 1 seeded and finely chopped red chile, 3 tablespoons finely chopped cilantro, and the finely grated rind of ½ lime. Stir in 3 cups cooked long-grain rice, mix, and spoon into bowls. Make the dipping sauce following the main recipe and serve warm, drizzled over the salad.

 Crab Fried Rice

Lightly beat 2 medium eggs with 1 tablespoon soy sauce and 1 teaspoon Thai fish sauce. Heat 2 tablespoons oil in a skillet and add half the egg, swirling to make a thin omelet. Cook for about 2 minutes, turning once, until slightly crispy. Remove from the skillet and roll. Repeat to make another omelet roll. Return the skillet to the heat with 2 tablespoons oil and add 3 chopped scallions, 1 seeded and chopped red chile, and a ¾-inch piece of fresh ginger root, chopped. Cook for 2–3 minutes, until soft. Stir 3 cups cooked mixed long-grain and wild rice into the skillet, along with ⅔ cup defrosted frozen peas. Cook for 2–3 minutes, then add 2 (6 oz) cans crabmeat, flaked, and cook for an additional minute, until hot. Spoon the fried rice into bowls, then thinly slice the egg rolls and sprinkle them over the rice. Serve drizzled with extra soy sauce.

30 Lemon Grilled Fish with Cheesy Mashed Potatoes

Serves 4

3 tablespoons chopped mixed herbs, such as chives, parsley, rosemary, and oregano

¼ cup olive oil

1 garlic clove, crushed

finely grated rind of 1 lemon

4 thick fish fillets, such as cod, haddock, or pollock (about 5 oz each)

8 medium potatoes (about 2 lb), such as russets, peeled and cut into chunks

2 tablespoons lemon juice

½ cup grated Parmesan-style cheese

salt and pepper

steamed green beans, to serve

• Mix 1 tablespoon of the chopped herbs and 1 tablespoon of the oil with the garlic, lemon rind, and a little seasoning, then rub over the fish fillets. Set aside for 10–15 minutes to marinate.

• Meanwhile, cook the potatoes in a large saucepan of lightly salted boiling water for 12–15 minutes, or until tender.

• Heat a ridged grill pan and cook the fish fillets, skin side down, for 4–5 minutes, until the skin is crispy. Turn the fish over, turn off the heat, and set aside for 3–4 minutes, until the fish is cooked. Keep warm.

• Drain the potatoes, return to the pan, and place over gentle heat for 1–2 minutes to dry them out. Add the lemon juice, cheese, remaining herbs, and remaining olive oil. Season with salt and pepper and mash until smooth, then spoon onto 4 warm plates. Serve the cheesy mashed potatoes with the grilled fish and steamed green beans.

---

10 Lemon, Shrimp, and Lima Bean Salad Rinse and drain 2 (15 oz) cans of lima beans and place in a bowl with 8 oz cooked, peeled shrimp, 3 tablespoons chopped fresh mixed herbs, the rind and juice of 1 lemon, 2 tablespoons olive oil, and plenty of seasoning. Toss gently to combine, then add 3 handfuls of arugula. Mound onto 4 shallow dishes and serve garnished with lemon wedges and Parmesan shavings, if desired.

20 Lemon-Mashed Lima Beans with Fish Place 2 (15 oz) cans drained and rinsed lima beans into a saucepan with 3 tablespoons chopped fresh mixed herbs, 1 crushed garlic clove, 2 tablespoons lemon juice, the finely grated rind of 1 lemon, and seasoning to taste. Add ½ cup hot vegetable stock and simmer gently, covered, for 10–15 minutes, until the beans are tender. Meanwhile, heat a large nonstick skillet and rub 1 tablespoon oil over the fish fillets. Season generously and cook, skin side down, for 4–5 minutes, until the skin is crispy. Turn the fish over and cook the other side for 2–3 minutes, until just cooked. Mash the beans with 2 tablespoons oil and ½ cup grated Parmesan-style cheese, then season to taste. Spoon onto 4 dishes and top with the fish, skin side up. Serve with steamed green beans, if desired.

Smoked Trout and Rice Noodle Salad

Serves 4

3 tablespoons vegetable oil
  or peanut oil
1 teaspoon Thai fish sauce
1 tablespoon lime juice
1 tablespoon light soy sauce
1 lb rice noodles, cooked and
  cooled
8 oz smoked trout pieces,
  cut into strips
1 bunch of fresh cilantro, chopped
1 red chile, seeded and chopped
1 small cucumber, finely sliced
1 red bell pepper, finely sliced

- Combine the oil, fish sauce, lime juice, and soy sauce in a jar with a tight-fitting lid and shake well to combine.

- Place the noodles in a large bowl with the remaining ingredients and toss with the dressing. Mound into 4 deep bowls and serve.

Hot-and-Sour Noodle Soup with Crispy Trout

Heat 5 cups stock in a saucepan with 3 tablespoons Thai fish sauce, 1 tablespoon rice vinegar, 1 tablespoon lime juice, and 1 tablespoon brown sugar. Add 1 seeded and chopped red chile, 1 tablespoon chopped fresh ginger root, and 1 sliced garlic clove. Simmer for 12–15 minutes. Meanwhile, heat 1 tablespoon sesame oil in a skillet and cook 4 trout fillets (about 4 oz each), skin side down, for 7–8 minutes. Turn and cook for an additional 1–2 minutes. Divide 1 lb rice noodles, cooked and cooled, among 4 bowls and pour over the broth. Top each with a fish fillet and serve sprinkled with chopped cilantro.

Marinated Salmon with Warm Noodle Salad

Place 4 salmon fillets (about 5 oz each), in a shallow ovenproof dish. Mix 1 tablespoon honey in a bowl with 1 tablespoon dark soy sauce, 1 tablespoon lime juice, 1 teaspoon Thai fish sauce, 1 seeded and finely chopped red chile, 1 crushed garlic clove, and 1 teaspoon finely grated fresh ginger root. Rub into the salmon and marinate for 12–15 minutes. Meanwhile, thickly slice 2 scallions, cut 1 carrot into matchsticks, and slice 1 red bell pepper. Place the salmon in a preheated oven, at 400°F, for 10–12 minutes, turning once, until just cooked. Remove and keep warm. Cook 8 oz thick dried rice noodles in a saucepan of lightly salted boiling water according to the package directions, until just tender. Heat 2 tablespoons oil in a large skillet, add the prepared vegetables, and cook for 3–4 minutes, until beginning to soften. Drain the noodles and toss with the vegetables, then mound into bowls and top with the salmon and any juices. Serve sprinkled with chopped cilantro.

 # Spaghetti with Broccoli, Lemon, and Shrimp

Serves 4

1 lb spaghetti

2 tablespoons olive oil

½ teaspoon dried red pepper flakes (optional)

8 oz cooked, peeled shrimp

grated rind and juice of 1 lemon

1 small bunch of basil leaves, shredded

5 cups small broccol florets

salt and pepper

handful of arugula, to serve

- Cook the spaghetti in a large saucepan of lightly salted boiling water according to the package directions, until al dente.

- Meanwhile, heat the olive oil in a small saucepan and warm the red pepper flakes for 1 minute, if using. Add the shrimp, lemon rind and juice, and basil leaves, season to taste, and heat through.

- Cook the broccoli in a small saucepan of lightly salted boiling water for 2–3 minutes, until beginning to soften slightly. Drain and add to the shrimp.

- Drain the pasta, return to the pan, and add the shrimp and broccoli mixture. Toss well to combine and mound into 4 shallow bowls. Serve topped with a little arugula.

Broccoli, Lemon, and Shrimp Salad

Blanch 5 cups broccoli florets in a small saucepan of lightly salted boiling water for 2–3 minutes, then cool under running water and drain. Make a dressing by combining 1 seeded and finely chopped red chile with 1 tablespoon lemon juice, 3 tablespoons oil, a pinch of grated lemon rind, and a little salt and pepper. Whisk to combine. Toss 1 (6 oz) package arugula with 8 oz cooked, peeled shrimp, 1 small bunch of basil leaves, shredded, 2 finely sliced scallions, and the broccoli and arrange on 4 plates. Drizzle with the dressing and serve.

 ### Broccoli and Shrimp Casserole

Cook 12 oz farfalle pasta in a large saucepan of lightly salted boiling water according to package directions, until al dente. Meanwhile, heat 4 tablespoons butter and ¼ cup flour in a saucepan with 2½ cups milk, stirring continuously, until thickened and smooth. Simmer for 1–2 minutes to cook the flour. Cook 5 cups broccoli florets in lightly salted boiling water for 2–3 minutes, until beginning to soften slightly, then drain and place in a large bowl with ½ teaspoon dried red pepper flakes, 12 oz cooked, peeled shrimp, 1 tablespoon lemon juice, and salt and pepper to taste. Stir

⅔ cup crème fraîche into the white sauce and add to the bowl with the drained pasta. Stir gently to combine, then pour into a large, ovenproof dish. Sprinkle with 2 cups fresh bread crumbs, drizzle with 1 tablespoon oil, and cook in a preheated oven, at 400°F, for 15–20 minutes, until bubbling and lightly golden. Serve with arugula, if desired.

BUD-FISH-GOT

30 Creamy Salmon and Spinach Phyllo Tarts

Serves 4

4 tablespoons butter, melted,
  plus extra for greasing
1 (10 oz) package frozen spinach,
  defrosted
¼ cup heavy cream
⅔ cup cream cheese
2 tablespoons chopped dill
  or chives
8 oz salmon fillet, cut
  into ½-inch cubes
8 phyllo dough sheets
  (about 10 x 8 inches)
hollandaise sauce, to serve
  (optional)
salt and pepper

- Preheat the oven to 400°F and lightly grease a baking sheet. Place the spinach in the middle of a clean dish towel, bring up the edges, and twist the spinach in the towel over a sink to squeeze out the excess moisture. Chop coarsely, then place in a bowl with the heavy cream, cream cheese, herbs, and seasoning. Mix well to combine, then gently fold in the diced salmon. Set aside.

- Brush both sides of the phyllo dough sheets with the melted butter. Place one sheet over another to form 4 crosses.

- Spoon the salmon mixture into the center of each dough cross and scrunch up the edges of the dough toward the filling, without completely covering it, to make 4 tarts.

- Transfer the tarts to the baking sheet and cook in the preheated oven for 12–15 minutes, until the pastry is golden and the fish is just cooked. Remove and serve drizzled with warm hollandaise sauce, if desired.

 Stylish Salmon and Spinach Baguettes

Drain 2 (6 oz) cans salmon and flake into a bowl. Add ¼ cup mayonnaise, 2 tablespoons chopped dill or chives, 2 teaspoons lemon juice, and some black pepper. Mash with a fork until combined and spread over the bottom halves of 4 mini baguettes. Top with 1 (5 oz) package baby spinach, then squeeze over extra lemon juice and season. Replace the lids and serve cut in half.

 Creamy Salmon and Spinach Puffs

Unroll 1 sheet ready-to-bake puff pastry and cut into quarters to make 4 rectangles. Brush with beaten egg and place on a greased baking sheet in a preheated oven, at 425°F, for 8–10 minutes, until golden and puffed up. Meanwhile, melt 4 tablespoons butter in a large saucepan and add 1 lb bite-size chunks of boneless, skinless salmon fillet. Cook for 2–3 minutes, turning occasionally, until lightly golden. Stir in ⅔ cup cream cheese, ⅔ cup heavy cream, 1 (10 oz) package defrosted frozen spinach, and 2 tablespoons chopped dill or chives, then season with a little salt and plenty of freshly ground black pepper. Simmer gently for 4–5 minutes, until the salmon is cooked, divide among 4 warm plates, and top each portion with a piece of pastry. Serve with baby spinach.

Spiced Mackerel and Couscous Salad

Serves 4

1¼ cups couscous
3 tablespoons olive oil
2 teaspoons harissa
1¼ cups boiling water
or vegetable stock
½ (15 oz) can mackerel fillets,
drained
½ red onion, finely sliced
1 small bunch of parsley,
coarsely chopped
8 cherry tomatoes, halved
1 small cucumber, seeded
and diced
2 tablespoons lemon juice
16 ripe black olives (optional)
salt and pepper

- Place the couscous in a bowl with ½ tablespoon of the olive oil, half the harissa, and a little salt and pepper. Stir with a fork until well coated. Pour over the measured boiling water or vegetable stock, then cover and set aside for 5–8 minutes, until the grains are tender and the liquid has been absorbed. Uncover, fluff with a fork, and transfer to a large, shallow bowl to cool.

- Meanwhile, flake the mackerel and toss together with the red onion, parsley, cherry tomatoes, and cucumber.

- Combine the remaining olive oil and harissa with the lemon juice. Season with salt and pepper and set aside.

- Fold the mackerel salad into the cooled couscous with half of the dressing and spoon into 4 shallow bowls. Serve sprinkled with the olives, if using, and drizzled with extra dressing.

 Quick Mackerel and Couscous Salad

Spoon 4 cups prepared couscous into 4 shallow bowls and flake 1 (15 oz) can mackerel fillets in spicy tomato sauce over the top. Sprinkle with 8 halved cherry tomatoes and chopped parsley, and serve.

 Harissa-Baked Mackerel with Couscous Use a sharp knife to make 3 slashes in each side of 4 whole scaled and gutted mackerel. Mix 1 tablespoon harissa with 1 tablespoon lemon juice, 1 tablespoon olive oil, and a little seasoning. Rub all over the mackerel and place in an ovenproof dish. Bake in a preheated oven, at 400°F, for 20–25 minutes, until the fish is cooked. Meanwhile, place 1¼ cups couscous in a bowl and stir in ½ tablespoon olive oil, 1 tablespoon harissa, and a little salt and pepper. Pour over 1¼ cups vegetable stock, cover, and set aside for 5–8 minutes, until the grains are tender and the liquid has been absorbed. Uncover, fluff up with a fork, and keep warm. Make a salad by combining ½ finely sliced red onion, 1 small bunch of parsley, coarsely chopped, 8 halved cherry tomatoes, 1 small seeded and diced cucumber, and 16 ripe black olives. Drizzle with 1½ tablespoons olive oil and 1 tablespoon lemon juice. Serve the spicy baked mackerel with the steamed couscous and the prepared salad.

1⏱ Lemony Tuna and Cranberry Bean Salad

Serves 4

grated rind and juice of 1 lemon

3 tablespoons olive oil

2 scallions, finely sliced

2 (5 oz) cans tuna in oil or spring
water, drained and flaked

2 (15 oz) cans cranberry beans,
drained and rinsed

1 small bunch of flat leaf parsley,
coarsely chopped

3 cups arugula

salt and pepper

- Combine the lemon rind and juice and olive oil and season with salt and pepper.

- Gently mix together all of the remaining ingredients and spoon into 4 shallow bowls. Drizzle with the dressing and serve immediately.

2⏱ **Seared Tuna with Warm Cranberry Beans** Heat 2 tablespoons olive oil in a skillet and cook 1 chopped red onion for 7–8 minutes. Add 2 (15 oz) cans cranberry beans, drained and rinsed, 1 bunch flat leaf parsley, chopped, and ½ cup vegetable stock. Season and simmer for 7–8 minutes. Rub 1 tablespoon oil over 4 small tuna fillets and season. Heat a ridged grill pan and cook the tuna for 3–4 minutes, turning once, until seared outside but pink inside. Set aside. Spoon the beans onto 4 warm plates and top each with a seared fish. Garnish with a few arugula leaves and squeeze the juice of 1 lemon over the fish to serve.

3⏱ **Grilled Tuna and Cranberry Bean Niçoise Salad** Rub 1 tablespoon oil over 2 tuna fillets (about 5 oz each), then season generously. Heat a ridged grill pan and cook the tuna fillets for 4–5 minutes, turning once, until almost cooked through. Remove, place in a dish, and set aside to cool for about 15 minutes. Boil 2 eggs in a small saucepan of water for 6 minutes, then cool under cold running water. Finely chop 1 green bell pepper and 1 small red onion, then seed and dice 3 ripe but firm tomatoes. Place in a bowl with 1 (15 oz) can cranberry beans, drained and rinsed, 1 small bunch of flat leaf parsley, coarsely chopped, and 3 cups arugula. Toss to combine, then divide among 4 plates. Shell the eggs and cut into wedges. Flake the tuna and arrange over the salads with the eggs. Drizzle with lemon juice and olive oil, and serve with crusty bread.

30 Nasi Goreng-Style Rice with Sardines

Serves 4

1⅓ cups long-grain rice

2 cups boiling water

⅓ cup vegetable oil,
plus extra for greasing

3 eggs

1 large onion, chopped

2 garlic cloves, chopped

3 tablespoons nasi goreng paste
or Thai chile paste

½ Chinese cabbage or 1 small,
green cabbage, shredded

2 tablespoons ketjap manis or
sweet soy sauce

4 (3¾ oz) cans sardines, drained
and flaked

4 oz cooked, peeled shrimp
(optional)

salt and pepper

½ cucumber, diced, to serve
(optional)

- Cook the rice in a large saucepan with the water according to the package directions, until the rice is tender and the liquid has been absorbed. Fluff with a fork to separate the grains, then spread over a large, lightly oiled baking sheet to cool.

- Meanwhile, beat the eggs in a bowl and season well. Heat 2 tablespoons of the oil in a large nonstick skillet and add half the beaten egg. Swirl the skillet so that the egg covers the bottom thinly. Cook for 30–60 seconds, until almost set, then flip over and cook the other side for 30 seconds. Slide out of the skillet and roll up tightly, then set aside to cool. Repeat with the remaining egg to make a second omelet.

- Heat the remaining oil in the skillet, add the onion and garlic, and cook for 7–8 minutes, until soft and lightly golden. Stir in the nasi goreng or Thai chile paste and stir-fry for 1 minute. Stir in the shredded cabbage and cook gently for 3–4 minutes, until soft, then stir in the ketjap manis or sweet soy sauce and half the sardines, mashing them into the vegetables. Stir in the rice and heat through. Once the rice is hot, add the shrimp, if using, and the remaining fish, folding gently to combine. Heat for an additional 2–3 minutes.

- Meanwhile, slice the omelets thinly and fold half the shredded omelet into the rice. Spoon the rice into 4 shallow bowls and top with the remaining sliced omelet and the diced cucumber, if using. Serve immediately.

 Broiled Nasi Goreng Sardines

Make 3 slashes in each side of 12–16 gutted and scaled sardines, and rub with 2 tablespoons nasi goreng or Thai chile paste. Arrange on a foil-lined broiler rack and cook under a preheated broiler for 4–5 minutes, turning once. Meanwhile, heat 3 tablespoons oil with 1 more tablespoon paste and add 3 sliced scallions and ½ shredded Chinese cabbage. Cook for 4–5 minutes, until soft, then stir in 3 cups cooked long-grain rice. Stir-fry for 2–3 minutes, then spoon onto 4 plates. Top each with 3–4 broiled sardines and serve garnished with ½ diced cucumber, if desired.

 Nasi Goreng

For this quicker version, use 3 cups already-cooked long-grain rice. Follow the main recipe but omit the omelets and instead fry 4 medium eggs in a hot skillet for 1–2 minutes, until slightly crispy. Serve one on top of each bowl of nasi goreng.

30 Crunchy-Topped Cod and Leek Pasta Casserole

Serves 4

2 tablespoons butter

3 tablespoons olive oil

4 oz bacon, chopped

2 leeks, thinly sliced

1 lb quick-cook fusilli

4 medium ripe tomatoes
(about 1 lb), diced

1 teaspoon finely grated lemon rind

2 tablespoons chopped herbs,
such as parsley, chives, basil,
rosemary, or oregano

1 lb skinless chunky cod, haddock,
or pollock fillet, cut into
bite-size pieces

2 tablespoons grated Parmesan-
style cheese

1⅔ cups fresh bread crumbs

salt and pepper

- Preheat the oven to 425°F. Melt the butter in a large, deep skillet with 1 tablespoon of the oil and cook the bacon for 2–3 minutes, stirring occasionally, until cooked and lightly golden. Add the leeks and cook for 2–3 minutes, stirring occasionally, until softened.

- Meanwhile, cook the pasta according to the package directions.

- Add the tomatoes to the bacon and leeks along with half the lemon rind and half the herbs, then season and simmer for 2–3 minutes, until the tomatoes begin to soften. Stir in the chunks of fish, then cover and simmer gently for 2–3 minutes.

- Meanwhile, mix the Parmesan with the remaining lemon rind and herbs and the bread crumbs, and season generously.

- Stir the drained pasta into the tomato sauce and transfer to a large ovenproof dish. Sprinkle over the bread crumb mixture, drizzle with the remaining oil, and bake in the preheated oven for 12–15 minutes, until the cod is cooked and the topping is crunchy.

10 Cod, Leek, and Bacon Arrabbiata

Heat 2 tablespoons oil in a skillet and cook 4 oz chopped bacon for 4–5 minutes. Add 1 lb skinless cod, cut into chunks, and 1 (12 oz) jar arrabbiata pasta sauce. Bring to a boil, reduce the heat, and simmer, covered, for 3–4 minutes. Heat 2 tablespoons butter in a saucepan and cook 2 sliced leeks for 6–7 minutes. Cook 1 lb quick-cook fusilli according to the package directions. Drain and divide among 4 bowls. Stir the leeks into the sauce and serve over the pasta.

20 Bacon-Wrapped Cod with Leeks

Cook 1 lb penne pasta according to the package directions, until al dente. Meanwhile, melt 2 tablespoons butter in a large, deep skillet with 1 tablespoon oil and cook 2 thinly sliced leeks for 5–6 minutes, until soft and golden. Add 4 medium diced ripe tomatoes (about 1 lb) to the leeks with ½ teaspoon finely grated lemon rind and 1 tablespoon chopped fresh mixed herbs, then season and simmer for 2–3 minutes, until the tomatoes begin to soften.

Rub 1 tablespoon oil over 4 skinless, boneless cod fillets, then season and wrap each one in 1–2 slices of bacon. Heat a nonstick skillet and cook the wrapped cod for 6–8 minutes, turning once, until both the cod and the bacon are cooked and lightly golden. Serve the cod on a bed of pasta with the tomato sauce, sprinkled with another tablespoon of herbs.

Garlic Breaded Salmon with Scallion Mashed Potatoes

Serves 4

8 medium floury potatoes (about 2 lb), such as russets, peeled and cut into chunks

3 day-old white bread slices, crusts removed

1 teaspoon dried garlic powder

2 tablespoons chopped mixed herbs, such as parsley, chives, and chervil

1 egg, beaten

2 tablespoons seasoned flour

4 skinless, boneless salmon fillets (about 5 oz each)

3 tablespoons vegetable oil

4 tablespoons butter

⅓ cup light cream

4 scallions, thinly sliced

salt and pepper

lemon wedges, to garnish

steamed broccoli, to serve

- Cook the potatoes in a large saucepan of lightly salted boiling water for 12–15 minutes, until tender.

- Meanwhile, place the bread in a mini chopper or food processor with the garlic and herbs, blend to create fine bread crumbs, and transfer to a plate.

- Pour the beaten egg into a shallow bowl and the seasoned flour onto a plate. Coat the salmon fillets in flour, then dip each fillet in the egg and turn to coat. Roll in the plate of garlicky bread crumbs until well coated.

- Heat the oil in a large nonstick skillet and cook the breaded salmon fillets for 6–7 minutes, turning once, until crisp and golden on the outside but still a little pink in the middle. Drain on paper towels and keep warm.

- Drain the potatoes and return to the pan with the butter and cream. Season well and mash until smooth. Stir in the scallions and spoon onto 4 warm plates. Top each mound with a crispy breaded salmon fillet, garnish with lemon wedges, and serve with steamed broccoli.

 Fried Salmon with Scallion Mashed Potatoes Heat 3 tablespoons oil in a large skillet and fry 4 skinless, boneless salmon fillets (about 5 oz each) for 7–8 minutes, turning once. Meanwhile, heat 1 (24 oz) package prepared mashed potatoes and stir in 4 sliced scallions. Crush 3 cups store-bought garlic and herb croutons in a mini chopper or food processor. Serve the salmon fillets with the mashed potatoes, sprinkled with the crushed croutons.

Healthy Garlic Salmon with Scallion Mashed Potatoes Follow the main recipe to coat 4 skinless, boneless salmon fillets in garlic bread crumbs. Place on a lightly greased baking sheet and bake in a preheated oven, at 375°F, for 15–20 minutes, until golden. Meanwhile, cook 8 medium floury potatoes (about 2 lb), such as russets, peeled and cut into chunks, in a large saucepan of lightly salted boiling water for 12–15 minutes, until tender. Drain the potatoes, return to the pan, and pour in ½ cup skim milk. Season well and mash until smooth, then stir in 4 thinly sliced scallions. Serve with steamed broccoli and lemon wedges.

QuickCook

Something Sweet

Recipes listed by cooking time

 # Chocolate and Nut Fondue

Serves 4

4 oz semisweet dark chocolate
4 oz milk chocolate
½ cup heavy cream
finely grated rind of 1 orange
3 tablespoons chopped
   mixed nuts

To serve

strawberries
shortbread or other plain cookies
marshmallows

- Place the chocolate, cream, and orange rind in a heatproof bowl over a saucepan of barely simmering water, so that the bowl is not quite touching the surface of the water. Let melt gently for about 10 minutes, then remove from the heat and stir until smooth.

- Meanwhile, toast the nuts in a small, dry saucepan over medium-low heat for 2–3 minutes, stirring frequently, until golden brown. Transfer to a plate and let cool slightly for 2–3 minutes.

- Pour the melted chocolate into a small fondue pot or attractive serving bowl and sprinkle with the toasted nuts. Serve with a choice of strawberries, cookies, and marshmallows for dipping, with 4 long fondue forks or metal skewers to spear them on.

 Chocolate Bar Fondue Place 1 (6 oz) Toblerone, or similar Swiss chocolate with nougat or nuts, broken into chunks, in a small saucepan with ½ cup heavy cream and a few drops of orange extract. Warm over low heat for 7–8 minutes, stirring occasionally, until melted and smooth. Pour into a fondue pot or bowl and serve immediately, with fruit, cookies, and marshmallows, following the main recipe.

 Decadent Chocolate-Dipped Fruit and Nuts Melt 8 oz semisweet dark chocolate in a heatproof bowl over a saucepan of barely simmering water, so that the bowl is not quite touching the surface of the water. Stir until smooth, then dip a combination of whole nuts (such as walnuts, almonds, pecans, and macadamias) and whole strawberries into the chocolate so that they are about two-thirds coated. Place on a baking sheet lined with parchment paper and chill in the refrigerator for 15–20 minutes, until hardened. Serve with espresso coffee.

30 Lime Cheesecake

Serves 4-6

2 cups crushed graham crackers
1 stick butter, melted
finely grated rind of 1 lime,
    plus 1½ tablespoons juice
1¼ cups cream cheese
⅔ cup confectioners' sugar
slices of lime, halved, to decorate

- Put the crushed cookies into a bowl and stir in the melted butter until well coated. Line the sides of a loose-bottom 8-inch cake pan with plastic wrap, then replace the bottom and press the cookie mixture evenly over the bottom of the pan. Chill in the refrigerator while making the filling.

- Meanwhile, place the lime rind and juice in a clean bowl with the cream cheese and confectioners' sugar and beat until smooth. Remove the cookie crust from the refrigerator, spoon over the filling, and smooth down with a spatula. Decorate with slices of lime. Return to the refrigerator for 20–25 minutes.

- Remove from the pan and gently peel away the plastic wrap. Cut into slices and serve.

1 Upside-Down Cheesecake

Mix together 2 cups crushed graham crackers and 1 stick melted butter until well coated. Beat the finely grated rind of 1 lime and 1½ tablespoons lime juice in a bowl with ½ cup Greek yogurt, ⅔ cup cream cheese, and ⅔ cup confectioners' sugar until smooth. Spoon into 4 attractive glass serving dishes and serve sprinkled with the cookie crumbs.

2 Lime Cheesecake Sandwiches

Place the finely grated rind of 1 lime and 1½ tablespoons lime juice in a bowl with 1¼ cups cream cheese and ⅔ cup confectioners' sugar and beat until smooth. Chill the cheesecake filling in the refrigerator for 15 minutes. Divide the mixture among 8 graham crackers, then top each one with a second graham cracker. Serve immediately.

30 Crunchy Baked Apples and Pears

Serves 4

3 (4 oz) containers apple pieces
  in juice
1 (15 oz) can pear slices in juice
½ cup applesauce
½ cup almond meal (ground
  almonds) or ground hazelnuts
½ cup chopped mixed nuts
2 cups fresh bread crumbs
¼ cup sugar
1 teaspoon ground cinnamon
  or allspice (optional)
4 tablespoons butter, melted
custard or whipped cream,
  to serve

- Preheat the oven to 400°F. Mix the apples and pears with the applesauce and transfer to an ovenproof dish.

- Mix the ground and chopped nuts with the bread crumbs, sugar, and spices, if using. Mix in the melted butter until well coated, then spoon the mixture over the fruit. Bake in the preheated oven for 20–25 minutes, until crunchy and golden. Serve hot with warm custard or whipped cream.

---

1 Apple and Pear Smoothie

Drain 3 (4 oz) containers apple pieces in juice and 1 (15 oz) can pear slices in juice, reserving the juice, and transfer to a blender with 1 coarsely chopped banana, a pinch of ground cinnamon, 1¼ cups of the reserved juice, and ½ cup Greek yogurt. Blend until smooth, then pour into 4 ice-filled glasses and serve immediately.

2 Crunchy-Topped Apple and Pear Sauce

Place ½ cup almond meal (ground almonds) or ground hazelnuts in a large, dry skillet with ½ cup fresh bread crumbs and 2 tablespoons sugar, and 1 teaspoon ground cinnamon or allspice, if using. Toast gently, stirring continuously, for 8–10 minutes, until golden. Transfer to a large, shallow bowl to cool. Meanwhile, drain 3 (4 oz) containers apple pieces in juice and 1 (15 oz) can pear slices in juice and blend in a food processor until smooth. Spoon into 4 individual glass serving dishes. Whip ⅔ cup heavy cream until thick and spoon over the pureed fruit. Sprinkle with the crunchy topping and serve.

20 Sweet Almond Frittata

Serves 4

5 extra-large eggs
1 cup confectioners' sugar
⅓ cup heavy cream
½ cup almond meal
(ground almonds)
1 teaspoon vanilla extract
(optional)
2 tablespoons butter
½ cup slivered almonds
vanilla ice cream or crème
fraîche, to serve

- Beat the eggs in a large bowl with ¾ cup of the sugar, the cream, almond meal, and vanilla extract, if using. Preheat the oven to 400°F.

- Melt the butter in a large, ovenproof skillet and pour in the egg mixture. Cook gently for 8–10 minutes, stirring occasionally, until the egg just begins to set. Sprinkle with the slivered almonds and the remaining confectioners' sugar, then place in the preheated oven for about 10 minutes, until set.

- Remove the skillet from the oven and cook under a preheated broiler for 2–3 minutes, until golden, then cool slightly and cut into slices. Serve with vanilla ice cream or crème fraîche.

 Sweet Almond Pancakes

Beat ½ cup almond meal (ground almonds), 1 teaspoon vanilla extract, and all but 2 tablespoons of 1 cup confectioners' sugar into 1 cup mascarpone. Divide the mixture among 4 small, store-bought pancakes, arrange in a large ovenproof dish, then top with another 4 pancakes. Sprinkle with ½ cup slivered almonds and the reserved sugar. Cook under a preheated broiler for 3–4 minutes, until warm and lightly golden.

 Sweet Almond Macaroons

Mix 1¼ cups almond meal (ground almonds) with ¼ cup sugar. In a separate large bowl, beat 2 extra-large egg whites with ½ teaspoon vanilla extract until stiff. Gently fold in the ground almond mixture until combined. Line 2 large baking sheets with parchment paper and place teaspoonfuls of the mixture on the baking sheets, allowing for room to spread. Bake in a preheated oven, at 350°F, for about 15 minutes, until just firm. Remove from the oven, let cool on the sheets for 3–4 minutes, then transfer to a wire rack to completely cool.

10 Strawberry Yogurt Crunch

Serves 4

¼ cup strawberry preserves or strawberry jam

3 tablespoons dark brown sugar

2 cups Greek yogurt

8 graham crackers

1 small chocolate-coated crunchy candy bar or chocolated-coated cookies, crushed, to decorate

- Spoon the strawberry preserves into the bottoms of 4 tall glasses. Stir the brown sugar into the Greek yogurt and divide half the mixture among the glasses.

- Place the graham crackers in a freezer bag and crush with a rolling pin, then use the crumbs to cover the yogurt. Spoon over the remaining yogurt and serve sprinkled with shards of chocolate-coated candy bars or crushed chocolated-coated cookies.

 20 Marinated Strawberry Crunch Chop 8 oz hulled strawberries and mix with 1 teaspoon lemon juice, 1 tablespoon brown sugar, and the seeds from ½ vanilla bean. Cover and set aside for 15 minutes. Place 8 graham crackers in a freezer bag and crush with a rolling pin, then divide the crumbs among 4 glass serving bowls. Top with 2 cups Greek yogurt, spoon the strawberries over the yogurt, and serve immediately.

 30 Strawberry Yogurt Crunch Muffins Mix 1 stick melted butter in a small bowl with ½ cup strawberry yogurt, 2 lightly beaten eggs, and 1 teaspoon finely grated lemon rind. In a large bowl, mix together ½ cup sugar, 1¼ cups all-purpose flour, ½ cup chopped almonds, 1 teaspoon baking powder, and ½ teaspoon baking soda. Pour the wet mixture into the dry ingredients and mix gently until just combined. Use to fill a 12-cup muffin pan lined with paper liners and sprinkle 1 extra tablespoon chopped almonds over the tops of the muffins. Bake in a preheated oven, at 350°F, for 18–20 minutes, until risen and golden. Cool slightly on a wire rack, then serve warm with strawberry preserves or jam, if desired.

BUD-SWEE-PYW

30 Creamy Vanilla Rice Pudding

Serves 4

⅔ cup short-grain rice
about 3 cups whole milk
¼ cup sugar
1 teaspoon vanilla extract or
   1 vanilla bean, split
2 tablespoons butter

- Place all the ingredients in a saucepan and bring to a boil. Reduce the heat and simmer gently for 25–28 minutes, stirring frequently and adding more milk, if necessary, until the rice is creamy and just tender.

- Remove the vanilla bean, if using, spoon the rice pudding into bowls, and serve immediately.

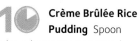 **Crème Brûlée Rice Pudding** Spoon 1 (22 oz) container prepared rice pudding into 4 individual ovenproof dishes. Sprinkle the surface generously with ¼ cup sugar, then cook under a hot broiler for 3–4 minutes, until the sugar begins to caramelize. Cool for a minute or two so that the sugar hardens, then serve immediately.

 Creamy Risotto-Style Rice Pudding Melt 4 tablespoons butter in a saucepan, add ⅔ cup short-grain rice, and cook, stirring, for 1 minute. Meanwhile heat 2½ cups milk to simmering point and stir in ¼ cup sugar and 1 teaspoon vanilla extract. Add the milk to the rice, a ladleful at a time, stirring continuously, until all the milk has been absorbed and the rice is al dente. This should take 17–18 minutes. Spoon into bowls, sprinkle each one with a little dark brown sugar, and serve.

Banana and Caramel Pancakes

Serves 4

4 prepared crepes (from a pancake mix) or 8 small store-bought pancakes

⅓ cup store-bought caramel sauce or dulce de leche, warmed

2 bananas, sliced

⅔ cup heavy cream

2 tablespoons coarsely grated semisweet dark chocolate or 2 chocolate-coated cookies, crushed

- Place the pancakes on 4 plates and drizzle with the caramel sauce. Sprinkle the sliced bananas over half of each pancake, then fold over to enclose or top with another 4 pancakes.

- Whip the cream to soft peaks, then place a spoonful on each pancake. Sprinkle with grated chocolate or crushed chocolate-coated cookies and serve.

Baked Caramel Banana Split

Place 4 large bananas on a baking sheet and cook in a preheated oven, at 350°F, for about 12 minutes, until blackened and soft. Meanwhile, gently warm ⅓ cup store-bought caramel sauce or dulce de leche in a small saucepan and whip ⅔ cup heavy cream to soft peaks. Remove the baked bananas from the oven and cut a slit down the center of each. Arrange in bowls and drizzle the warm sauce over the bananas. Spoon the whipped cream over the bananas, sprinkle with the chocolate, and serve.

Warm Banana-Caramel Muffins

Beat together 1 stick softened butter, 1 cup all-purpose flour, ⅔ cup sugar, 2 teaspoons baking powder, and 2 eggs in a bowl. Mash 1 large, ripe banana and fold into the mixture. Use to fill a 12-cup muffin pan lined with paper liners and bake in a preheated oven, at 350°F, for about 20 minutes, until risen and golden. Meanwhile, warm ⅓ cup caramel sauce or dulce de leche in a small saucepan, and whip ⅔ cup heavy cream to soft peaks. Serve the warm muffins in a bowl, drizzled with the warm sauce and accompanied by a spoonful of whipped cream.

 # Melting Chocolate Desserts

Serves 4

4 oz semisweet dark chocolate

1 stick butter, plus extra for greasing

⅔ cup sugar

2 eggs

2 tablespoons unsweetened cocoa powder

3 tablespoons all-purpose flour

confectioners' sugar, for dusting

- Preheat the oven to 350°F and butter 4 large ramekins, about 3¼ inches in diameter. Melt the chocolate and butter in a small saucepan over low heat.

- Meanwhile, beat together the sugar and eggs, and pour in the melted chocolate. Beat in the cocoa powder and flour, and continue beating until smooth.

- Divide the mixture among the ramekins and cook in the preheated oven for 10–12 minutes, or until crisp on top and still melting inside.

- Remove from the oven, set aside to cool for 1–2 minutes, then serve dusted with confectioners' sugar.

---

10 Vanilla Ice Cream with Melting Chocolate Sauce Melt 6 oz semisweet dark chocolate with 1 tablespoon maple syrup, 1 tablespoon butter, and ¼ cup water in a heatproof bowl over a saucepan of barely simmering water, so that the bowl is not quite touching the surface of the water. Warm until melted, then mix until smooth and glossy. Serve drizzled over vanilla ice cream.

30 Dark Chocolate Soufflés Melt 4 oz semisweet dark chocolate in a heatproof bowl over a saucepan of barely simmering water, so that the bowl is not quite touching the surface of the water. Heat gently until melted but not hot. Whisk in 3 egg yolks, then fold in ⅓ cup plus 1 tablespoon all-purpose flour and ½ teaspoon baking powder. Whisk the 3 egg whites in a large bowl with ¼ cup sugar to form soft peaks. Gently fold the whisked egg whites into the chocolate. Lightly grease 4 individual ovenproof dishes or ramekins and place on a baking sheet. Divide the mixture among them and cook in a preheated oven, at 375°F, for 12–15 minutes, until well risen. Serve immediately, dusted with confectioners' sugar.

30 Caramel Apples

Serves 4

1 stick butter

1 tablespoon dark brown sugar

1 teaspoon lemon juice

3 apples, such as Golden Delicious or Pippin, peeled, cored, and cut into 8 slices each

16 sheets of phyllo dough

For the caramel sauce

2 tablespoons butter

¼ cup dark brown sugar

2 cups heavy cream

- Preheat the oven to 350°F and line a baking sheet with parchment paper. Melt half the butter in a skillet with the sugar and lemon juice. Add the apples and cook for 8–10 minutes. Meanwhile, melt the remaining butter and brush over 4 sheets of phyllo dough. Top each buttered side with a second sheet of dough. Brush again with butter and repeat until all the sheets are used to form 4 stacks of phyllo.

- Remove the apples from the saucepan, reserving the pan and its juices. Divide the apples among the sheets of dough, arranging them at one end. Fold the other end of the dough over the top to cover the apples. Turn in the edges and fold them over to create 4 packages. Arrange on the baking sheet and cook in the preheated oven for 12–15 minutes.

- Meanwhile, make the caramel sauce by placing the butter, brown sugar, and heavy cream in the skillet. Stir over low heat until the sugar has melted, then bubble for 1–2 minutes, until thick and deep golden. Remove from the heat to cool.

- Remove the apple packages from the oven and serve drizzled with caramel sauce.

1 Apple Skewers

Melt 4 tablespoons butter in a saucepan with ¼ cup heavy cream and ¼ cup packed dark brown sugar. Stir until the sugar dissolves, then simmer for 1 minute. Remove from the heat and set aside. Peel and core 4 apples, such as McIntosh, and cut into chunks. Toss in 1 teaspoon lemon juice. Thread the apple onto 8 small skewers and arrange on serving plates. Add a scoop of vanilla ice cream to each plate and drizzle with the caramel sauce.

2 Caramelized Apple Layer

Peel, core, and cut 3 dessert apples, such as Pippin, into ¾-inch dice. Melt 4 tablespoons butter in a large skillet with 1 tablespoon dark brown sugar and 1 teaspoon lemon juice. Add the apples and cook for 8–10 minutes, turning occasionally, until softened and golden. Remove from the heat and cool slightly. Meanwhile, crush 8 gingersnaps in a freezer bag with a rolling pin until they resemble fine bread crumbs and mix with 4 tablespoons melted butter to combine. Spoon the apples and cookie crumbs into 4 serving glasses in layers, and top each one with a small scoop of ice cream or Greek yogurt and a sprinkle of sugar. Serve immediately.

30 Old-Fashioned Rock Cakes

Serves 4

2 cups all-purpose flour

1½ tablespoons baking powder

1 teaspoon allspice

1 stick cold butter, diced

½ cup raw sugar or granulated sugar, plus extra for sprinkling

1 teaspoon grated orange rind (optional)

¾ cup mixed dried fruit

¼ cup candied peel, chopped candied cherries, or extra mixed dried fruit

1 extra-large egg, beaten

3–4 tablespoons milk

- Preheat the oven to 350°F and line a baking sheet with parchment paper. Place the flour, baking powder, and allspice in a food processor with the butter and pulse until the mixture resembles fine bread crumbs. Transfer to a large bowl, then stir in the sugar, orange rind, if using, dried fruit, and candied peel.

- Pour in the beaten egg and add enough milk to bind the mixture to a soft, slightly sticky dough.

- Use 2 forks to make 8 rocklike mounds of the dough on the prepared baking sheet. Sprinkle with a little extra sugar and cook in the preheated oven for 18–20 minutes, until the rock cakes are golden and a toothpick inserted into the middle comes out clean. Transfer to a wire rack to cool a little before serving.

1 Rock Cake Yogurt

Place ¾ cup mixed dried fruit and ¼ cup candied peel or chopped candied cherries in a small saucepan with 1 teaspoon grated orange rind, ¼ cup orange juice, ½ teaspoon allspice, and 2 tablespoons light brown sugar. Warm gently, stirring occasionally, until the sugar has dissolved. Set aside to cool slightly, then spoon the fruit mixture into 4 individual glass dishes. Top each dish with ½ cup Greek yogurt, then crumble a soft amaretti cookie or shortbread cookie over the yogurt to serve.

2 Banana, Raisin, and Cinnamon

Mini Rock Cakes Sift 2 cups all-purpose flour with 1½ tablespoons baking powder and ½ teaspoon ground cinnamon. Rub in 1 stick diced cold butter until the mixture resembles fine bread crumbs, then stir in 1 small mashed banana and ⅓ cup raisins. Bind with 1 extra-large beaten egg and a little milk, if necessary, then arrange 16–20 small spoonfuls of the mixture on a large baking sheet lined with parchment paper. Cook in a preheated oven, at 375°F, for 8–10 minutes, until cooked and golden, then transfer to a wire rack to cool.

30 Spiced Shortbread Squares with Caramel Ice Cream

Serves 4

1¼ sticks butter

⅓ cup sugar, plus extra for rolling

1⅔ cups g all-purpose flour

½–1 teaspoon ground cinnamon
or allspice

4 scoops of caramel ice cream

- Preheat the oven to 350°F and line a baking sheet with parchment paper.

- Place the butter and sugar in a food processor and blend until well mixed. Add the flour and spice and blend to just combine. Invert onto a smooth surface and knead lightly to form a soft dough.

- Shape into a 6-inch-long cylinder and roll in the extra sugar. Flatten the sides slightly, so the dough has a square cross section. Cut into approximately 16 square slices and place on the prepared baking sheet. Cook in the preheated oven for about 15 minutes, until lightly golden.

- Transfer to a wire rack to cool slightly, then serve warm with scoops of caramel ice cream.

 1 Caramel and Shortbread Ice Cream Crumble 12 shortbread cookies into 4 individual glass serving dishes. Top each with a scoop of vanilla ice cream and drizzle with a tablespoon of warm caramel sauce or dulce de leche. Sprinkle each serving with 1 tablespoon chocolate chips and serve immediately.

 2 Chocolate-Covered Shortbread Melt 8 oz orange-flavored semisweet dark chocolate in a heatproof bowl over a saucepan of barely simmering water, so that the bowl is not quite touching the surface of the water. Dip one-half each of 12 shortbread cookies in the melted chocolate. Arrange on a baking sheet lined with parchment paper and chill in the refrigerator for 10–15 minutes. Serve with scoops of chocolate ice cream.

30 Ginger and Syrup Cake

Serves 4

¾ cup light corn syrup
 or golden syrup
1 stick soft butter or margarine,
 plus extra for greasing
⅔ cup sugar
2 eggs
1 cup all-purpose flour
1½ teaspoons baking powder
1½ teaspoons ground ginger
light cream or custard,
 to serve

- Preheat the oven to 350°F and grease an ovenproof dish. Pour the corn syrup into the bottom of the dish.

- Place all of the remaining ingredients in a bowl and beat until smooth, then pour the batter over the corn syrup. Smooth with a spatula to make an even layer, then cook in the preheated oven for 20–25 minutes, until risen and golden.

- Serve drizzled with cream or warm custard.

 Quick Ginger and Molasses Cake
Place 1 tablespoon molasses in a small saucepan with 4 tablespoons butter, ⅓ cup packed light brown sugar, 1½ teaspoons ground ginger, and ½ cup heavy cream. Heat until the sugar has dissolved and the mixture is smooth and glossy. Arrange 4 slices of warm pound cake on 4 serving plates, then drizzle with the ginger and molasses sauce and serve with cream, if desired.

 Ginger Syrup Cookies Beat
1 stick softened butter in a bowl with 1 egg, 1½ teaspoons ground ginger, 3 tablespoons light corn syrup, and ¼ cup granulated sugar or raw sugar. Add 1⅓ cups all-purpose flour and 2 teaspoons baking powder and mix to combine. Place spoonfuls of the dough on a large baking sheet lined with parchment paper, allowing for room to spread, and bake in a preheated oven, at 350°F, for about 10 minutes, until golden. Cool on a wire rack and serve.

20 Cherry Tiramisu

Serves 4

⅓ cup confectioners' sugar, sifted
½ cup strong black coffee
12 ladyfingers
1 cup mascarpone or cream
  cheese
⅔ cup heavy cream
2 tablespoons crème de cassis
  or syrup from canned cherries
1 (15 oz) can black cherries
  in light syrup, drained

- Stir 2 tablespoons of the confectioners' sugar into the coffee. Arrange the ladyfingers in the bottoms of 4 individual glass dishes, then pour over the black coffee and set aside to soak for about 5 minutes.

- Meanwhile, beat the remaining confectioners' sugar into the mascarpone and heavy cream with the crème de cassis or cherry syrup. Spoon over the ladyfingers and chill in the refrigerator for 10–15 minutes. Spoon the drained cherries on top to serve.

 Quick Cherry Tiramisu Divide 1 (12 oz) can of cherry pie filling among 4 individual glass serving dishes. Beat the cream with 1¼ cups Greek yogurt and 1 tablespoon honey until thickened, then crumble 6 ladyfingers into the mixture. Spoon onto the cherry filling and serve dusted with unsweetened cocoa powder.

---

3 Golden Baked Cherries and Pears Drain and chop 1 (14½ oz) can pear slices in juice and put into an ovenproof dish with 1 (15 oz) can black cherries, drained. Place 6 tablespoons butter in a food processor with 1⅔ cups all-purpose flour and 2½ teaspoons baking powder and pulse until the mixture resembles fine bread crumbs. Add ¼ cup sugar and

⅔ cup Greek yogurt, then pulse to just combine. Spoon the mixture over the cherries and pears and cook in a preheated oven, at 400°F, for 20–25 minutes, until golden. Serve with cream, if desired.

3. Carrot Cake Scones with Cream Cheese

Serves 4

1⅔ cups all-purpose flour

3½ teaspoons baking powder

½ teaspoon ground cinnamon

½ teaspoon ground nutmeg

pinch of salt

4 tablespoons butter, plus extra
 for greasing

¼ cup sugar

½ cup peeled and shredded carrot

⅓ cup raisins

1 teaspoon finely grated
 orange rind

2–3 tablespoons milk,
 plus extra for brushing

For the cream cheese filling

⅔ cup cream cheese

3 tablespoons confectioners'
 sugar, sifted

1 teaspoon vanilla extract
 (optional)

- Preheat the oven to 425°F and lightly grease a baking sheet. Mix the flour in a bowl with the baking powder, ground spices, and salt. Rub in the butter until the mixture resembles fine bread crumbs, then stir in the sugar. Stir in the grated carrot, raisins, and orange rind, then add enough milk to make a soft dough.

- Knead very lightly on a lightly floured surface, then pat flat to a thickness of ¾ inch. Cut into about 8 triangles, using up any remaining dough to make more scones. Place on the prepared baking sheet and brush with a little milk. Cook in the preheated oven for about 12 minutes, until risen and golden.

- Meanwhile, make the filling. Beat the cream cheese in a bowl with the confectioners' sugar and vanilla extract, if using, until smooth. Set aside.

- Remove the scones from the oven and cool slightly on a wire rack. Slice the warm scones in half, spread cream cheese on one half, then reassemble and serve.

 Fruit Scones with Cream Cheese

Warm 4–8 prepared fruit scones in a preheated oven, at 350°F, for 3–4 minutes. Meanwhile, beat ⅔ cup cream cheese in a bowl with 3 tablespoons sifted confectioners' sugar and 1 teaspoon vanilla extract, if using, until smooth. Serve the cream cheese filling with the warm scones.

 Quick Carrot Cake Scones

Place 1 (14 oz) package plain scone mix in a large bowl, add ⅓ cup raisins, ½ cup shredded carrot, ½ teaspoon ground cinnamon, and ½ teaspoon ground nutmeg, and mix according to the package directions to make a dough, adding an extra splash of milk, if necessary. Knead lightly on a lightly floured surface, then pat flat to a thickness of ¾ inch and cut into about 8 triangles. Place the scones on a lightly greased baking sheet and bake in a preheated oven, at 425°F, until golden and cooked. Slice and butter the scones while still warm.

1 ⏱ Lemon Tart with Vanilla Cream

Serves 4

1 cup lemon curd or prepared
lemon pie filling

1 prepared piecrust, about
9 inches across

8 oz strawberries, hulled and
sliced

1 vanilla bean, split lengthwise

1 cup heavy cream

1 tablespoon confectioners' sugar

- Spread the lemon curd over the bottom of the piecrust, then sprinkle with the sliced strawberries.

- Scrape the seeds from the vanilla bean into the cream with the confectioners' sugar and whip until it forms soft peaks. Spoon over the strawberries and serve immediately.

2 ⏱ Lemony Vanilla Fool

Divide ½ cup lemon curd or prepared lemon pie filling among 4 individual glass serving dishes. In a large bowl, beat 1 cup Greek yogurt with 1 cup mascarpone, the seeds from 1 vanilla bean, and ½ cup more lemon curd or lemon pie filling. In a separate bowl, whip 1 cup heavy cream until it forms soft peaks, then fold gently into the lemony mascarpone. Spoon the mixture into the glasses and chill for 10 minutes before serving with crisp cookies.

3 ⏱ Lemon and Vanilla Mousse

Place 1 cup heavy cream, the seeds from 1 vanilla bean, the grated rind of 1 lemon, and ¼ cup sugar in a large bowl and whip until it forms soft peaks. Whisk 2 egg whites in a clean bowl until stiff and fold gently into the cream with ¼ cup lemon curd or lemon pie filling. Spoon ¾ cup lemon curd or lemon pie filling into 4 tall serving glasses, then top with the mousse. Chill in the refrigerator for 15–20 minutes, or until ready to serve.

BUD-SWEE-ZEZ

30 Pear and Walnut Muffins

Serves 4

2 cups all-purpose flour
½ cup packed dark brown sugar
1 teaspoon baking powder
¾ teaspoon baking soda
½ teaspoon ground cinnamon
½ cup walnut pieces, chopped
1 cup plain yogurt
4 tablespoons butter, melted
2 extra-large eggs, beaten
2 canned pear halves in juice,
  diced
2 tablespoons honey, warmed,
  to serve (optional)

- Preheat the oven to 350°F. Mix together the dry ingredients in a large bowl. Beat the remaining ingredients together in another bowl. Now pour the wet ingredients into the dry and stir with a large spoon until just combined.

- Use the batter to fill a 12-cup muffin pan lined with paper liners and bake in the preheated oven for 15–18 minutes, until risen and golden. Cool a little on a wire rack, then serve drizzled with warm honey, if desired.

 Warm Honeyed Pears with Walnuts

Place 4 tablespoons butter, 2 tablespoons honey, and ½ teaspoon ground cinnamon in saucepan, and warm gently until melted and smooth. Drain 2 (14½ oz) cans pear slices in juice, then arrange in shallow bowls. Pour over the warm buttery honey and serve sprinkled with the walnut pieces.

 Cinnamon-Baked Pears with Walnuts

Gently warm 4 tablespoons butter, 2 tablespoons honey, and ½ teaspoon ground cinnamon in a saucepan until melted and smooth. Meanwhile, peel, halve, and core 4 ripe but firm pears and place, cut sides down, in a snug-fitting ovenproof dish. Sprinkle with ½ cup chopped walnuts, drizzle with the warm sauce, and bake in a preheated oven, at 375°F, for 15 minutes, until warm through and slightly softened. Serve with store-bought muffins, if desired.

30 Ginger and Lemon Cupcakes

Serves 4

½ cup peanut oil or vegetable oil
½ cup plain yogurt
2 eggs, lightly beaten
1 teaspoon finely grated lemon
  rind, plus extra to decorate
½ cup sugar
1¼ cups all-purpose flour
1 teaspoon ground ginger
1 teaspoon baking powder
½ teaspoon baking soda
confectioners' sugar, to decorate

- Preheat the oven to 350°F. Place all the ingredients in a large bowl and beat well until smooth.

- Use the batter to fill a 12-cup muffin pan lined with paper liners and bake in the preheated oven for 15–18 minutes, until risen and golden. Cool on a wire rack and serve warm or cold, decorated with a sprinkling of confectioners' sugar and finely grated lemon rind.

10 Ginger and Lemon Cheesecakes

Crush 16 gingersnaps cookies in a freezer bag with a rolling pin and mix the crumbs with 2 tablespoons melted butter until well coated, then divide among 4 individual glass ramekins, pushing down with the back of a spoon to cover the bottoms. Beat together 1 teaspoon finely grated lemon rind, ⅔ cup Greek yogurt, ⅔ cup cream cheese or mascarpone, and 1–2 tablespoons honey, according to taste. Spoon into the ramekins and serve.

20 Ginger and Lemon Fruit Gratin

Drain 2 (15 oz) cans peaches in juice and arrange in an ovenproof dish. In a bowl, beat together 1½ cups Greek yogurt, 1 teaspoon finely grated lemon rind, 1 teaspoon ground ginger, and 2 tablespoons dark brown sugar. Spoon the mixture over the fruit and smooth the surface. Sprinkle with another 2 tablespoons dark brown sugar and cook under a preheated moderate broiler for 7–8 minutes, until the sugar has melted and is beginning to caramelize. Cool slightly, then spoon into bowls to serve.

30 Buttery Brioche Dessert

Serves 4

4 tablespoons butter, softened,
  plus extra for greasing
8 thick slices of brioche
3 eggs, beaten
¼ cup sugar
2 cups whole milk
1 teaspoon vanilla extract
  (optional)
½ cup golden raisins
light cream, to serve (optional)

- Preheat the oven to 350°F and grease a large ovenproof dish. Spread butter over both sides of each brioche slice. Heat a nonstick skillet and sauté the brioche slices for 1–2 minutes on each side, until crisp and golden.

- Beat together the eggs, sugar, milk, and vanilla extract, if using.

- Arrange the brioche slices in the prepared ovenproof dish, sprinkle with golden raisins, and pour over the egg mixture. Cook in a preheated oven for 20–25 minutes, until just set and lightly golden. Serve with light cream, if desired.

 Buttery Brioche with Ice Cream Spread both sides of 8 thick brioche slices with softened butter, then sprinkle with ¼ cup sugar. Heat a nonstick skillet and sauté the brioche slices for 1–2 minutes on each side, until crisp and golden. Cut into triangles and arrange on serving plates with scoops of vanilla ice cream and sprinkled with ½ cup golden raisins.

 Golden Brioche with Homemade Custard Pour 2½ cups whole milk into a saucepan with 1 teaspoon vanilla extract and heat to boiling point, then remove from the heat. Meanwhile, beat 4 egg yolks in a large bowl with ¼ cup sugar and 2 teaspoons cornstarch. Beat the hot milk into the eggs, then return the mixture to the pan and warm over low heat, stirring continuously, until thickened, being care not to let the mixture boil. Remove from the heat and keep warm. Meanwhile, toast 8 slices of brioche in butter and sprinkle with the sugar, following the 10-minute recipe. Cut into triangles, arrange in bowls sprinkled with golden raisins, and serve drizzled with warm custard.

30 Fallen Fruit Crisp

Serves 4

2 apples, such as Pippin, peeled,
cored, and cut into wedges

2 pears, such as Bosc, peeled,
cored, and cut into wedges

1½ cups fresh or frozen
blackberries

2 tablespoons orange juice

½ cup light brown sugar

6 tablespoons butter, softened

1 cup all-purpose flour

3 tablespoons rolled oats

1 teaspoon ground allspice

2 tablespoons honey

1 cup Greek yogurt

- Preheat the oven to 400°F. Place the fruit in a large saucepan with the orange juice and 2 tablespoons of the sugar, and warm over medium heat for 4–5 minutes, stirring occasionally, until the fruit begins to soften.

- Meanwhile, rub the butter into the flour until the mixture resembles fine bread crumbs, then stir in the remaining sugar, the oats, and half the allspice.

- Transfer the fruit to an ovenproof dish and sprinkle with the topping. Cook in the preheated oven for about 20 minutes, until golden.

- While the crisp is in the oven, stir the honey and remaining allspice into the yogurt and chill until required. Serve the fruit crisp hot with the spiced yogurt.

---

1 **Fallen Fruit Granola** Peel and core 2 apples, such as Pippin, and 2 pears, such as Bartlett. Cut into wedges and place in a large saucepan with 1½ cups fresh or frozen blackberries, 2 tablespoons orange juice, and ½ cup light brown sugar. Warm over medium heat for 4–5 minutes, stirring occasionally. Once the fruit has softened slightly, spoon into dishes and top each one with ½ cup store-bought crunchy granola. Serve with the spiced yogurt, as above.

2 **Forest Fruit Crunch** Place 4 cups frozen mixed fruits in a saucepan with ¼ cup sugar and 1 teaspoon finely grated orange rind. Warm until the fruit has defrosted and the sugar dissolved, then pour into an ovenproof dish. Meanwhile, crush 12 oatmeal cookies in a freezer bag with a rolling pin and mix with 1 teaspoon ground allspice and ¼ cup slivered almonds, if desired. Sprinkle the topping over the fruit and cook in a preheated oven, at 400°F,

for about 10 minutes, until hot and golden. Serve dusted with confectioners' sugar, with spoonfuls of the spiced yogurt, as above.

 # Almond Affogato

Serves 4

4 scoops of nougat or vanilla
ice cream
4 drops of almond extract
4 shots of hot strong coffee
1 tablespoon slivered almonds,
toasted
almond cookies, to serve
(optional)

- Place a scoop of ice cream into each of 4 heatproof serving glasses. Stir the almond extract into the hot coffee, then pour 1 shot over each scoop of ice cream. Sprinkle with the toasted almonds and serve with almond cookies, if desired.

 ### Affogato-Inspired Cookies Beat

1¼ sticks softened butter and 1¼ cups sugar together until pale and creamy, then beat in 1 teaspoon coffee extract and 1 egg. Add 2 cups all-purpose flour, ½ teaspoon baking soda, and 1 cup chopped almonds and mix to combine. Arrange 16–20 small spoonfuls of the dough on 2 large, lightly greased baking sheets, allowing for room to spread. Cook in a preheated oven, at 350°F, for 6–8 minutes, until lightly golden. Transfer to wire racks to harden and cool slightly. Serve with ice cream and strong espresso coffee.

 ### Affogato-Style Tiramisu

Stir 4 drops of almond extract into ½ cup cold strong coffee. Arrange 16 ladyfingers in a dish, then pour the coffee over them and set aside for 5 minutes to soak. Break up the ladyfingers and divide half of them among 4 tall, freezer-proof glasses. Spoon a small scoop of nougat or vanilla ice cream into each of the glasses, and top with the remaining ladyfingers. Top with another small scoop of ice cream, then place in the freezer for 10–15 minutes, until firm. Sprinkle with a dusting of unsweetened cocoa powder and 1 tablespoon toasted slivered almonds and serve with almond cookies or thin wafers, if desired.

Raspberry Ripple Pain Perdu

Serves 4

1 (10 oz) package frozen
  raspberries
1 teaspoon lemon juice
2 tablespoons confectioners'
  sugar, plus extra for dusting
2 eggs, lightly beaten
⅔ cup sugar
1 teaspoon vanilla extract
  (optional)
1 cup whole milk
4 thick slices of day-old bread
  or brioche
6 tablespoons butter
crème fraîche, to serve (optional)

- Place the raspberries in a saucepan with the lemon juice and confectioners' sugar, and warm very gently until just beginning to collapse. Blend in a food processor until smooth then pass through a strainer to remove the seeds.

- Beat together the eggs, sugar, and vanilla extract, if using. Add the milk slowly, beating until smooth and incorporated.

- Dip the slices of bread in the egg mixture, so that both sides are well coated. Melt the butter in a large nonstick skillet and cook the egg-coated bread slices gently for about 2 minutes on each side, until crisp and golden.

- Remove the bread from the skillet and arrange on serving plates. Drizzle with the warm raspberry coulis to create a ripple effect, then dust with confectioners' sugar and serve immediately with crème fraîche, if desired.

10 Pain Perdu with Raspberry Ripple Ice Cream Follow the main recipe to coat 4 thick slices of day-old bread or brioche in the egg mixture, and sauté the bread slices until golden. Remove from the skillet and sprinkle both sides of the bread with raw sugar or granulated sugar. Arrange on serving plates and top each slice with a scoop of raspberry ripple ice cream and a dusting of confectioners' sugar.

30 Baked Raspberry Pain Perdu Cut 4 thick slices of day-old bread or brioche into cubes and arrange in an ovenproof dish. Beat 2 eggs with 1 extra egg yolk, ⅔ cup sugar, 1 teaspoon vanilla extract, and 1 cup whole milk, and pour over the cubes of bread. Sprinkle with 1 cup fresh raspberries, and cook in a preheated oven, at 350°F, for about 20 minutes, until just set and golden. Serve dusted with confectioners' sugar, with crème fraîche, if desired.

 # Almost Instant Peach Trifle

Serves 4

4 individual strawberry shortcake rolls, sliced

1 (15 oz) can peach slices in juice, drained, juice reserved

1 cup mascarpone

1 cup prepared vanilla pudding

2 tablespoons confectioners' sugar

⅔ cup heavy cream, whipped

3 tablespoons grated chocolate, to decorate

- Use the shortcake roll slices to line the bottom of an attractive glass serving dish. Drizzle ½ cup of the reserved juice over the slices, then sprinkle with the peach slices.

- Beat the mascarpone with the vanilla pudding and confectioners' sugar, and spoon it over the fruit.

- Spoon the whipped cream over the pudding mixture, and decorate with the grated chocolate.

2 Orange Flower Poached Peaches

Cut 6 ripe but firm peaches or nectarines in half and remove the pits. Place in a saucepan with 2 cups water, 1 cup orange juice, 1 teaspoon orange flower water, and 2 tablespoons confectioners' sugar. Bring to a boil, then reduce the heat and simmer gently for 8–10 minutes, until tender. Pour into a large, shallow bowl and set aside to cool. Meanwhile, beat 2 teaspoons orange flower water into the mascarpone with 2 extra tablespoons confectioners' sugar. Spoon the poached peaches into 4 bowls with as much of the cooking liquid as desired. Serve with the mascarpone and 8 ladyfingers.

3 Baked Peaches with Mascarpone

Cut 6 ripe but firm peaches or nectarines in half and remove the pits. Place the peaches, cut sides up, in a snug-fitting ovenproof dish. Mix ½ cup orange juice with 2 tablespoons honey and pour over the peaches. Sprinkle over 2 tablespoons confectioners' sugar and cook in a preheated oven, at 350°F, for 15–18 minutes, until tender. Meanwhile, beat 2 tablespoons confectioners' sugar into the mascarpone and chill until required. Remove the peaches from the oven and arrange in serving dishes. Sprinkle with 1 cup fresh raspberries, if desired, and serve with the mascarpone.

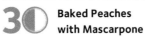

Giant Orange and White Chocolate Chip Cookies

Serves 4

1¼ stick soft butter or margarine,
   plus extra for greasing
1¼ cups sugar
finely grated rind of 1 orange or
   1 teaspoon orange extract
1 egg
2 cups all-purpose flour
pinch of salt
½ teaspoon baking soda
4 oz white chocolate,
   cut into chunks

- Preheat the oven to 350°F and lightly grease 2 nonstick baking sheets. Beat the softened butter and sugar together until pale and creamy, then beat in the orange rind or extract and the egg. Sift the flour, salt, and baking soda into the bowl and mix to combine. Stir in the chocolate chunks.

- Arrange 6 large spoonfuls of dough on each of the 2 prepared baking sheets, allowing plenty of room for the dough to spread. Cook in the preheated oven for 10–12 minutes, until lightly golden.

- Transfer to wire racks to harden and cool slightly. Serve warm or cold. Any leftover cookies can be stored in an airtight container for 2–3 days.

White Chocolate and Orange Hot Chocolate Coarsely grate 8 oz white chocolate and place in a heatproof bowl. Heat 3 cups milk in a saucepan with 1 teaspoon orange extract until it just reaches boiling point, then pour it over the grated chocolate. Stir until completely melted, then divide among 4 mugs. Top each serving with a spoonful of whipped cream and extra white chocolate curls, if desired, and serve with store-bought white chocolate cookies.

White Chocolate Blondies Melt 12 oz white chocolate and 6 tablespoons butter in a small saucepan over gentle heat and set aside. Meanwhile, break 3 eggs into a bowl with ⅔ cup sugar, 1 teaspoon orange extract, and the finely grated rind of 1 orange and beat with a wooden spoon. Stir in the melted chocolate, 1¼ cups all-purpose flour, and 2 teaspoons baking powder, then pour into a lined and greased brownie pan, about 9 inches square. Cook in a preheated oven, at 350°F, for about 20 minutes, until golden and slightly risen but not too firm. Cool slightly, then cut into squares and serve warm with white chocolate or vanilla ice cream.

BUD-SWEE-PEO

Index

Page references in *italics*
indicate photographs

Acknowledgments

Executive editor: **Eleanor Maxfield**
Senior editor: **Leanne Bryan**
Copy-editor: **Jo Smith**
Art director: **Jonathan Christie**
Design: **Tracy Killick**
Art direction: **Juliette Norsworthy & Tracy Killick**
Photographer: **Bill Reavell**
Home economist: **Denise Smart**
Stylist: **Isabel De Cordova**
Senior production controller: **Caroline Alberti**